Master Georgia Kiafi

Chinese almanac 2025

The ultimate guide for a successful year

Year of the Snake

Master Georgia Kiafi
Chinese almanac 2025 -
The ultimate guide for a successful year
The year of the Snake

Author
Georgia Kiafi
Rutiweg 1,
8604 Volketswil, Switzerland
Mobile: +4179 788 79 48
Email: georgiakiafi@hotmail.com
Website: www.thefengshuilife.com
Facebook page: The Feng Shui Life (articles in English)
Blog: georgiakiafi.blogspot.com (articles in Greek)

Copyright © 2025 by Georgia Kiafi

All rights reserved. No part of this publication may be reproduced, stored in a retrieval system, or transmitted, in any for or by any means, electronic, mechanical, photocopying, recording or otherwise, without the prior permission of the copyright owner.

CONTENTS

Preface   page 4-7

Feng Shui 2025
Flying Stars for the year   page 8-29
Flying Stars for the month   page 30-33
Grand Duke   page 34-37
Clash   page 38-39
3 shars   page 39-40
Earth Shars   page 41
Flying Grand Duke   page 42
Li Shih   page 43

Renovation & construction
- where to avoid construction in the year   page 44
- where to avoid construction each month   Page 45-47
- where to avoid construction each day   page 48
- where and when to start construction   page 48-53
- Choosing the right day to start construction   page 54-55
- Days and hours to avoid Feng Shui consultation   page 55

Grand Duke Talisman 2025   page 56

4 pillars of destiny 2025
Predictions 2025 and more
World predictions   page 58-71
Predictions for the 12 Chinese animals   page 72-75
Predictions for the 10 day masters   page 76-85

Date Selection 2025
9 steps to success   page 88
Clash   page 89
12 Rulers   page 90-94
Influence   page 94-95
Good and bad activities   page 96
Flying Star of the day   page 96
Nobleman   page 97-98
Favourable elements & 10 Gods   page 98
3 Shar & Death Angel   page 98-99
How to select the hour   page 99-103

Tong Shu 2025
About the Tong Shu   page 106-107
Tong Shu & days   page 108-199
Tong Shu & hours   page 200-211

Appendix
Your chinese animal sign   page 212
Correcting the hour - solar time for major cities   page 213-214

About the author
Georgia Kiafi bio   Page 216

Preface

We are getting into the year of the snake. According to the Chinese Solar Calendar, 2025 is the year of the wood snake. It starts the 3rd of February 2025 and it finishes the 3rd of February 2026. Wood, fire and their interaction will be the main elements of the new year which will affect our lives in every single aspect.

The "Chinese Almanac 2025" is a useful tool that will help you in many ways to get the best out of the year.

The first part of the book contains Feng Shui tips about the year 2025. Most people have heard about Feng Shui and know some basic Feng Shui rules such as how to find the best position of the bed in the bedroom.

Few people however know that Feng Shui has a time dimension. Although we have our bed at the same position for many years, not every year is the same. Some years we get sick or have trouble, and some other years things go very well. Why is that?
Actually, every direction of our space, home or business, is influenced by invisible energies called Flying Stars. Flying Stars theory is a very important school of Feng Shui. Flying Stars have a specific pattern in the way they move around space and time, their movement can be calculated. Your bed, main door and office desk are the most important areas to check.

In my "Chinese Almanac 2025" you will learn where the yearly and monthly Flying Stars are located. You will be able to reduce effectively all the negative Flying Stars of 2025 such as those that can cause misfortune, sickness, arguments or even burglary. You will know where are the good energies that can help romance, academic success and money luck.

Feng Shui is not the only aspect that influences our lives. Feng Shui by itself usually it cannot kill us. What we call Chinese Astrology also plays a huge role together with the luck that we create with our own choices. The Chinese in their cosmology speak about the trinity of luck, which is Heaven (examined by astrology), Man (the luck we create ourselves) and Earth (examined by Feng Shui).

This book cannot replace a Feng Shui consultant. To do things properly, one needs to examine the exact Feng Shui of a space by using the special Chinese compass called Lo Pan and lots of formulas. However, the "Chinese Almanac 2025" can help you "DIY" the Feng Shui of your space with some good results. I have a special chapter about renovations, as digging at the wrong direction may cause trouble. As such, I also give the solutions where and when to dig and renovate when you really have to do so.

I wrote this book having in mind people that are new in Feng Shui, but I stretched the knowledge to the level that it can be used by Feng Shui students and professionals alike. You only need to read it throughout carefully if you are new to the subject.

In the "Chinese Almanac 2025" I also included predictions for world events. As 2025 is the year of the wood snake this energy is going to influence world events. Using Chinese astrology, you may already know how the new year will operate. It is good to be prepared and not to leave things in luck, Chinese believe that nothing is random, everything that happens has a pattern. Also Albert Einstein said "God does not play dice". Why should you "play" your life on a dice? Knowledge and good preparation are both essential for success.

Each one of us belongs to a Chinese animal, there are in total 12 Chinese animals. Most people know if they were born in the year of the tiger, rabbit, dragon etc. I have included some Chinese animal predictions in this book; however, it is important to make clear that predictions based in the year animal of birth is not very accurate. Not everybody born in the same year will have the same events.

The system of Chinese astrology called "4 pillars of destiny" or "BaZi" talks about the "Day Master". Day Master or "heavenly stem of the day" or "personal element" is the element that was predominant in the day of birth of the specific month of the specific year of a person. We find this information in the Chinese Calendar which is a book that is like an ephemeris.

There are in total 10 Day Masters; yang and yin wood, yang and yin fire, yang and yin earth, yang and yin metal, yang and yin water. You may find your personal Day Master in online BaZi calculators.
Predictions based on the Day Master are much more accurate than the Chinese animal predictions. Of course, it is best to ask a specialist to check your complete "4 Pillars of Destiny" chart as there is so much more info to be considered.

2025 is a year with a very special meaning, as it marks the beginning of seeing fire during Period 9 (Period 9 lasts for 20 years). From 2024 until 2044 we are under the influence of the element of fire. We are going to see huge changes in all levels of our society, as fire and its characteristics will be the driving power for everything.

Another aspect of the "Chinese Almanac 2025" is Date Selection. Many of us have important activities to do during the new year such as moving house, sign contracts, get married etc.

As not everyone knows how to do Date Selection, I have included many pages with the most important Date Selection formulas so that you can Do It Yourself.

Not every hour has the same energy. Many cultures around the world have a saying that "what cannot be brought in a year, it can be brought in an hour". After correcting the hour of our watch to the solar hour, we can find the best hours to do important things for every day. Towards the end of the book you will find an easy reference table that show the good, fair and bad hours of each day of the year. I also give the formulas to make a more specialized hour selection based on your Chinese animal and your Day Master.

The "Chinese Almanac 2025" is an almanac that I publish since many years now. It is my vision to help people improve their lives considering the different factors of Feng Shui, 4 Pillars of Destiny (Chinese Astrology) and Date Selection. I hope you enjoy it.

Blessings
Master Georgia Kiafi
www.thefengshuilife.com

Feng Shui 2025

Flying Stars for the year
03 February 2025 - 03 February 2026 – the year of wood snake

Flying stars is a Feng Shui school that examines the time dimension. It is energy that is located in a direction for a specific period of time and brings specific effects, there are total 9 types of energies called Flying Stars. The Flying Stars for easy reference are numbers from 1 to 9, each number means something and belongs to an element, colour, shape, season, family member etc.

There are flying stars for the year, for the month, for the day and for the hour. There are also flying stars that are permanent since the birth and occupation of the building. There is even a flying star grid that predominates for 20 years called Age or Period.

You may know the permanent flying stars of your home or business only via a Feng Shui consultant. A professional can put all the information together after measuring the exact degrees of your house facing and considering the time period of first construction and occupation.

In this book we only examine the flying stars for the year and month.

Check if any bad flying stars are visiting your bed, bedroom door, office, cashier if you have a shop, apartment door, even building entrance.
This is the grid of the Flying Stars of the year.
Please note that the new year is always starting around the 4 th of February, depending on the year. It is not starting the 1st of January like in the West.

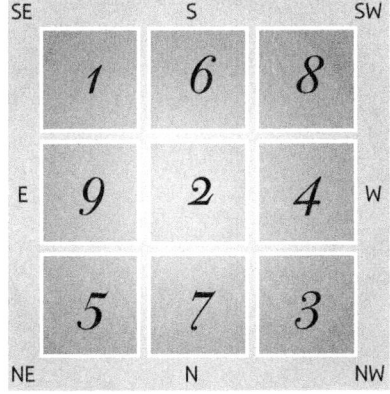

Flying Stars 2025 - the year of wood snake
03 February 2025 - 03 February 2026

After the new year comes in, the new flying star influences come in. This means that until the beginning of the new year in February, you keep the old Feng Shui remedies for the previous year. After the beginning of the new year, only then you do the remedies I mention on this book.

Read below what you can do in 2025 at each direction of your house, office or shop. I suggest that you take a normal compass (always try to stay away from metals etc.) and find the 8 directions from the center. Find where is east, west, southwest etc.

Flying star 1 in the Southeast - coming prosperity & academic success

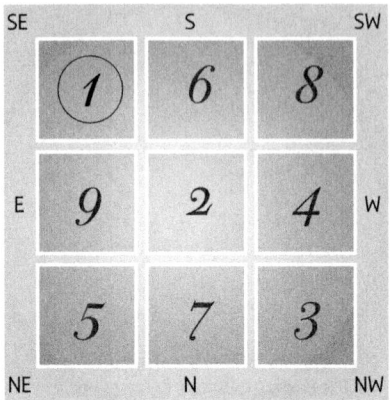

Flying star 1 can help you with recognition and connectivity. It belongs to water element, water connects people and moves goods, water is synonymous to trading as it moves things around.

It also brings wisdom and academic advancement as it is an academic star. It helps exchanging information with people, without people you cannot obtain wisdom, you gather information from people and you get wisdom. It brings intelligence, good name, fame, social position, and of course it helps with travel. It is the middle son. Its related to sea life, shipping industry, liquids, the drinks industry, it's the abyss.

If you want to improve academic success and receive the benefits of the yearly flying star 1, you can sit inside the location of Flying Star 1, or just face towards that direction. Or combine both, sit inside it and face it at the same time. However, I do not suggest you with easy heart to activate flying star 1 by sitting there, facing it, or by putting active objects like water fountain, TV & radio, pendulum clock, or by using a lot of black, white, wavy shapes and water.

This is because you do not know the original flying star chart of your house of office. If bad flying stars are there and the star 1 comes, this can cause you a lot of dangerous situations.

If flying star 1 is together with bad stars you will experience these things: scandals, be cheated by people, fall in a trap, getting drowned, having floods or water disasters or lose reputation.

It can bring depression and emotional disturbance, isolation, darkness, solitude, theft, commit suicide, death, become alcoholic. It's the graveyard.

Its also related to sexual organs, it's the semen, the ear and can affect the kidneys.

Activate flying stars 9, 1, 2, 4 only if you know the original flying star chart of your space through a Feng Shui consultant, unless you want to experiment.

Flying star 2 in the Center - sickness

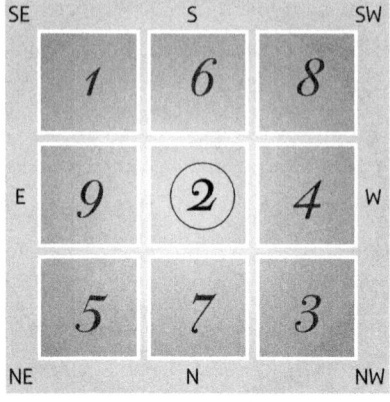

Although we are into Period 9, the Flying Star 2 is still causing sickness. Only towards the end of Period 9 it will become a positive star. Other negative traits of Flying Star 2 is that its making people submissive, passive, pessimist, coward and dull. It causes depression, stinginess and loneliness. It can cause fertility issues, miscarriage, cancer, intestine & stomach problem, even diabetes, chronic illness and fatigue.

If you are sleeping on it, or if your main door is located where the Flying Star 2 resides, you will be affected by it, getting one of the issues I describe above.

It also affects you if you spend a lot of time at its location. For example, if you are spending a lot of time at your office desk or favorite sofa and the Flying Star 2 is there, you will also feel its results.

It is best to avoid being located where the 2 is located. But if you cannot avoid it, for example if your bed is there and you cannot sleep somewhere else, or if your main door is there and you have no other way to get into your apartment, then you have to use Feng Shui remedies that reduce its influence. Flying Star 2 is considered the second worse Flying Star after Flying Star 5, as health is so important in our life.
The most typical remedy to reduce the effect of Flying Star 2 is a string of 6 coins or a metal gourd. Let us look into these Feng Shui remedies more deeply.

String of 6 coins
This Feng Shui remedy is based on the 5 elements. As Flying Star 2 belongs to earth element, a string of 6 coins is about using metal element as much as possible. Metal coins belong to metal. You may use a copper, red or gold coin, as copper and gold are yang, silver is yin. Yang is stronger than yin, so in overall we prefer coins made of "yang" material. We may also use numbers, as numbers represent elements too. Number 1 represents water element, water is weakening the earth effect of Flying Star 2. In Europe, the 1 cent is copper color (yang), it is metal material, and 1 represents water. When we take 6 of them, we use even more metal element this way, as 6 is a yang metal element number. So, if you want to make your own Feng Shui remedy for Flying Star 2, take 6 copper color coins of value of 1 eurocent, and tape them together, one next to the other, to form a string. Then your string of 6 coins is ready to use and put it at the location of Flying Star 2.

You may buy the string of 6 coins ready prepared for you from a shop that sells Feng Shui items. If you want to make the extra mile with your 6 coin string, instead of the existing red thread that connects the Chinese coins, you may replace it with a black, gold or even silver thread. This is because red is fire element, fire is not good as it supports the earth element of Flying Star 2. So its best to incorporate more metal and water element using the appropriate color.

A metal gourd
In the old times, Chinese doctors were putting medicine into gourds. Flying Star 2 is about sickness, so symbolically we can use a gourd to reduce the sickness start 2.
However, if you observe better, a gourd has a metal shape, it has many round shapes at different spots. Round shape is metal, exhausting the earth element of Flying Star 2.

It is best to invest in a metal Chinese gourd, as metal material is helping even more into the effectiveness of reducing the sickness star 2.

This is what you can do at the sector with the yearly Flying Star 2;
- Avoid spending much time at the location of Flying Star 2, as it affects your health.
- Use metal and water color in big scales (white, silver, gold, black, dark blue).
- Place a string of 6 metal coins or a metal gourd to reduce its effect.
- Avoid having too much fire element in that sector. For example avoid too much red or purple, avoid using your fireplace or using candles at the affected area.
- Avoid facing it, especially if you already have health issues.
- Make sure you don't have too many triangular shapes at that location. Also look for such shapes at the exterior environment, such as sharp corners for other roofs and buildings.
- Avoid sets of objects that relate to fire element. Number 9 is fire element, so avoid having sets of 9 sets of objects.

Feng Shui remedy for star 2

Feng Shui remedy for star 2

Flying star 3 in the Northwest - arguments

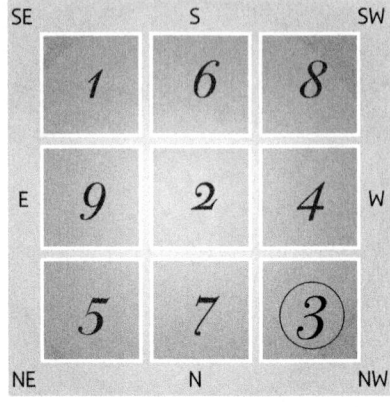

Flying star 3 can bring arguments. It may also bring hot temper, gossip, aggressivity, back stabbing, being unpolite, misunderstandings, disagreements, lawsuits.

It may affect the liver, legs and walking ability. It brings surprise and is uncontrolled. (like thunder).

Flying star 3 may help you if you are a sportsman, fighter, or working in a very competitive environment where constant growth, bravery and keep fighting is important, but usually 3 has more of the negative effects. So ask yourself if you really want it or you prefer to reduce it. Flying star 3 is wood element.

If you are sleeping on it, sitting on it or facing it, you have more chances to have such effects. It may also influence you when you do renovations there. It also affects you if your office desk is there, or your own apartment or building door. It is the 4nd worse flying star after star 5.

Avoiding star 3 is again the best thing you can do. But if you cannot avoid it, for example if you cannot move your bed or use another door, you may do Feng Shui remedies. Remedies reduce the power of negative flying stars but they cannot make them totally disappear.

Things can still happen, but they just happen in smaller scale. Remedies

use shape, material, number and colour, exactly with this priority. Eg using shape is more effective that colour, unless strong colour is covering a huge surface.
This is what you can do at the sector with the yearly flying star number 3:

- Use fire colour in big scales (red, purple, firy orange etc). Eg hang a big red painting, place many red pillows – see photos of this page
- Use your fireplace more if it happens to be located in that sector.
- Put candles and use them.
- Earth element is also good, eg yellow color, stones, crystals, sand, ceramics.
- Avoid activity in that location, thus avoid playing the TV or music for hours.
- Avoid renovations, constructions, digging earth.
- Avoid facing it
- Make sure you don't have any ugly, wavy or oblong objects outside your house at this sector.
- Avoid sets of object that come in numbers of 3, 4, or 1. For example avoid 3 flags or any 3 things together. 3, 4 is wood, 1 is water.

Flying star 4 in the West - sex scandals & academic star

Flying star 4 is related to arts, academics and beauty. It makes people like you because they find you attractive. It belongs to wood element, it is known as peach blossom. Just like a graceful flower, you know how to be flexible, you move according to the wind, it makes you pleasant. People like you and they give you their knowledge, they feel that as a sensitive flower you need protection. It is the image of a pen for calligraphy. Public recognition.

Thus its also an academic star but different than star 1. It helps you think fast, react fast, being adaptive. It's the flowers, ivy and the grass. It can help you appeal beautiful and graceful, it can help you with arts. It can be used by artists, students, academics, painters, graphic designers etc and bring success in these star 4 related activities. It's the first daughter, the wind, it affects the hips and the liver. It's the books, the artist brush, contracts, the rope, the school and the post office.

One way to receive the effect of any Flying star is to be inside its location and spend time in it, especially when you do an activity that is related to that star. For example, if you want to improve your attractivity to opposite sex or your artistic talent, you can sit inside the location of Flying Star 4. Another way is that you face that star when you are sitting, so that star 4 is in front of you in straight line. Or you may combine both, sit inside and face it at the same time. However, I do not suggest you easily to activate flying star 4 or to receive it by sitting on it or by facing it. Other ways to activate it is by putting real active water, a vase with water and fresh flowers, put active objects like TV music or pendulum clock, or use wood and water colors like green blue black. Ugly objects outside your house like an ugly mountain or ugly building they can also activate the bad character of star 4.

Although Flying Star 4 can make you very likable and increase your appeal to the opposite sex and even bring you many new flirts, it does not guarantee that you will be happy with this situation, nor it guarantees the quality of those flirts.

Maybe you will become the third party in a marriage, or to have people flirting with you but none is interesting. I think you get the point. Flying star 4 is not auspicious during Age 9 (2024-2044) and brings easily its bad effects too.
It can bring sexual scandals, superficial relationships, immorality, being lazy, being too relaxed, get into alcohol and adultery.
As flying star 4 is related to the wind trigram of the I Ching and wind changes direction all the time, the person can also be wandering without purpose, without targets. As star 4 is related to a rope, it can bring asphyxia, to be struggled, even hanging.

So be careful and think twice before you activate star 4, as flying star 4 is not timely nor positive during age 9 (we are currently at age 9 from 2024-2044), if your personal space has other bad stars there together with star 4 you risk to have its negative effects.

If you want to suppress star 4, use fire element in that sector, put real candles and use them regularly, use fire colours such as red or purple colour, avoid activity there by using the TV etc.

Flying star 5 in the Northeast - misfortune

Flying star 5 brings trouble and misfortune. 5 belongs to earth element, its like lava earth and its the strongest earth.

If you are sleeping on it, sitting on it or facing it, you will feel its bad influence this year. It is also activated if at that location you have a lot of activity (TV, pendulum clock, music) or when you do renovations there. It is also bad if this year your apartment door or building door is located there.
It is the worse star of all.

Avoiding star 5 is the best. But if you cannot avoid it, for example if you cannot move your bed or use another door, you may use remedies. Remedies can reduce the power of negative flying stars but cannot make them disappear. Things can still happen, just in smaller scale.
Remedies use shape, material, number and colour, exactly with this priority. Eg using shape is more effective that colour, unless strong colour is covering a huge surface.

This is what you can do at the sector with the yearly flying star number 5:
- Water salt cure (put a glass with 1/3 thick salt, 1/3 water, on the salt you place in circular manner 6 coins of cupper, golden colour, in the center you place 1 silver colour coin) – see photo of this page
- Avoid fire colours, especially in big surfaces. Avoid red, purple, firy orange etc.
- Avoid activity in that location, thus avoid playing the TV or music for hours.
- Avoid renovations, constructions, planting tree, digging earth.
- Avoid facing it
- Make sure you don't have any ugly or sharp (fire) objects outside your house at this sector.
- Avoid sets of 9, for example avoid 9 flags or any 9 things together. 9 is fire.
- Prefer metal and water colours and shapes. Put a metal windchime or other metal objects. Use black, grey, white, metallic colors, use round oval and wavy shapes.

Flying star 6 in the South - legal trouble & authority

Flying star 6 is related to power and authority. It's the emperor and the king. It's the government, the manager and the CEO, it is someone with a higher social position that was obtained after hard work. Star 6 can also help with discipline and courage.

It is the star of military arts. it creates a sudden result and moves with one go and cannot be stopped (unlikely star 3). Even if it has military power, it rules with justice. It's the star of morality, determination, authority, longevity, devotion and progress, leadership and achievement. It belongs to metal element and it's the heaven trigram. Flying star 6 governs the lungs and the head. It's the father and the old man.

One way to receive the effect of any Flying star is to be inside its location and spend time in it. For example, if you want to improve your authority or discipline, you can sit inside the location of Flying Star 6. Another way is that you face that star when you are sitting, so that star 6 is in front of you in straight line. Or you may combine both, sit inside and face it at the same time.

However, during age 9 (years 2024-2044) flying star 6 is not positive any more. Once you spend time in it, or you activate it with active water, TV, radio etc, or even you put there fire elements (red, triangle shapes etc) or you spend a lot of time inside the area of flying star 6, or if you face it, it can bring you a lot of problems.

It can create problems with the authorities or the government, legal problems, dominance, headache, injuries on the head, loneliness, losing power, becoming retired, sudden fall, violent death, traffic accidents. Being strong headed, isolation, sadness, leaving the home of the family.

This is why I would not activate the flying star 6, instead I would suppress it with water and,or wood element, for example I would put there a transparent glass vase with real water and fresh bamboos ideally in numbers of 3, 4 or 1.

I might put green, black, blue in that area, and I would definitely avoid reds in big scale. I would especially do that if I anticipate legal troubles that year.

Flying star 7 in the North - scandals

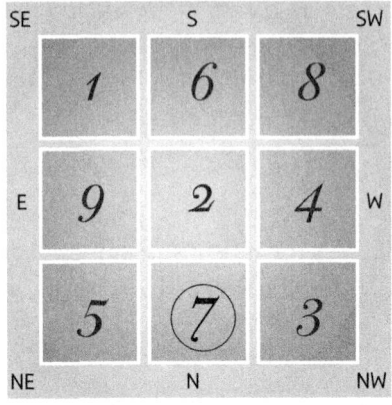

Flying star 7 can bring scandals. It also brings robbery, fake flattery, assassin, con artist, unwanted attention and making noise, magic, poison, tricky negotiation (under the table), wrong talking and verbal fight, blackmail, cuts on the skin, losing voice, teeth, sex desease. It affects fertility and pregnancy (too yin), injury by knife or sharp object, being bitten by the mouth of an animal, medical operation problem of speech, imprisonment or even fire. It is also related to the mouth and the younger daughter. Men can cheat their wife because they find a sweet talking woman.

Flying star 7 may help you if you are a lawyer (it attracts lawsuits), singer, public speaker, surgeon, tv presenter, mystic,witch, depending on the flying star chart and layout of your space, but usually 7 has more of the negative effects. Flying star 7 belongs to metal element.

If you are sleeping on it, sitting on it or facing it, you have more chances to have such effects. It may influence you when you do renovations there. It is not good if your office desk or apartment door is there. It is the 3nd worse flying star after star 5.

Avoiding star 7 is again the best thing you can do. But if you cannot avoid it, for example if you cannot move your bed or use another door, you may do Feng Shui remedies. Remedies reduce the power of negative flying stars but cannot make them disappear. Things can still happen, just in smaller scale. Remedies use shape, material, number and colour, exactly with this priority. Eg using shape is more effective that colour, unless strong colour is covering a huge surface.

This is what you can do at the sector with the yearly flying star number 7:
- Vase with water and 3, 4 or 1 pieces of bamboo or other green plant. The vase must be transparent glass, not ceramic - see photos of this page
- Avoid fire colours in big surfaces, thus avoid red, purple etc.
- Avoid activity there, avoid TV or music playing, avoid moving water.
- Avoid renovations, constructions, digging earth.
- Avoid facing it.
- Make sure you don't have any ugly or sharp (fire) objects outside your house at this sector.
- Avoid sets of 9, for example avoid 9 flags or any 9 things together. 9 is fire, fire activates the bad character of star 7.
- Prefer wood and water colours and shapes. Use black, dark grey, green, blue, use tall,oblong and,or wavy shapes reminding wood and water.

Flying star 8 in the Southwest - past prosperity

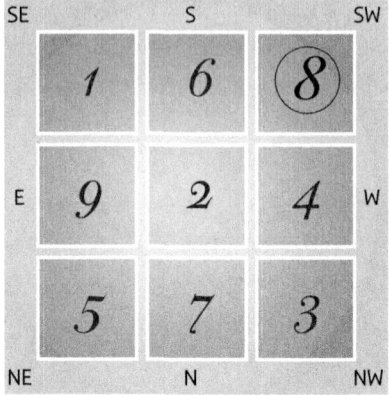

Flying Star 8 is not prosperous any more since we entered Period 9 in 2024.

Flying Star 8 has the following negative keywords: loneliness, stubborn, stingy, greedy, lazy, reserved, loss of prosperity, conflict about inheritance, children get hurt, joint and hand injury.

If you are sleeping on It, or if your main door is located where the Flying Star 8 resides, you will be affected by it, getting one of the issues I describe above.

It also affects you if you spend a lot of time at its location. For example, if you are spending a lot of time at your office desk or favorite sofa and the Flying Star 8 is there, you will also feel its results.

Flying Star 8 although it is not prosperous any more, it does not have such a bad character by itself if you compare it to the presently main negative flying stars 5, 2, 7 and 3.

Flying Star 8 is one of the so called "white" stars, together with star 1 and 6, meaning that the original character of these stars are not so bad and they are not causing such huge disaster, even when they are not very prosperous. However, in some cases they can cause trouble, so its better to keep an eye on it.

Myself, I do not focus so much to treat the Flying Star 8 using Feng Shui remedies, unless I experience some trouble directly related to it.

It belongs to earth element, so the best way to reduce it is by applying metal and water element.

You may reduce the effect of Flying Star 8 by doing the following:

- Apply metal and/or water colors, such as white, gold, silver, black, dark blue.
- Use metal and water shapes in your furniture or decorations, such as wavy/asymmetrical shapes (water element) or/and oval/curves (metal element).
- Metallic objects such as metallic decorative statues, collection of coins will help reduce the earth energy of Flying Star 8.
- Use objects that come in sets of 1 (water), 6 (metal) or 7 (metal).
- Avoid active objects such as water fountain, swimming pool, TV, pendulum clock etc.
- Avoid too much fire element, do not use candles, fireplace, red or purple color etc.

Flying star 9 in the East - current prosperity, celebration and attention

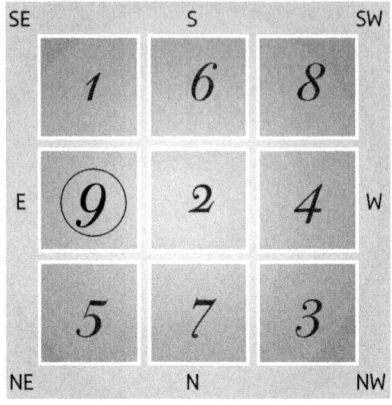

Flying star 9 is related to happy events, good news, celebrations, progress, warmth, passion, popularity, glory, talent in expression, communication, light, good mood, attention and shine.

It's the star of beauty. It wants to show its talents to the world, it wants to draw the attention of the world. It belongs to the fire element, it is the eyes.

Fire is the source of light, it shines light into the darkness and is the source of hope. Its when energy is at its maximum, like burning flames. It is a romantic star that leads to marriage, it is full of energy that pushes you to work. It can bring amazing success and progress. It makes things happen from one moment to the other. Its about spiritual things that do not exist physically.

It rules the eyes and the heart. It is the middle daughter, so it helps especially women. One way to receive the effect of any Flying star is to be inside its location and spend time in it. For example, if you want to improve your warmth and popularity or money prosperity, you can sit inside the location of Flying Star 9 or to face it... Or you may combine both, sit inside and face it at the same time.

However, I am not suggesting to energize annual flying star 9, unless you know the other flying stars of your house or business located there (you can find out from your Feng Shui consultant). If you choose to receive its effects, sit on it or face it.

You may also activate it by using active objects there, such as a water fountain, swimming pool, TV & radio, pendulum clock if it's a living room or entrance, or even sleep on it so that it can affect your personal relationships according to its character.

Flying star 9 energizes the other stars located at the same sector, it has a "ghostly" nature so it can make the good better and the bad worse.

Baring this in mind, I also mention to you the negative effects of flying star 9. It can cause depression, a step backwards in life and career, a feeling of disatisfaction, the person cannot neither express itself nor communicate. Easy to have misunderstandings from what the person says to the others, bad mood, show off, difficulty to find a job.

Star 9 has to do with the eyes, the heart but also the mind (brain intelligence). so when negative it creates health problems with the eyes and the heart, affects badly the way of thinking, the person is doing strange things in order to draw attention. It can create heated arguments and emotional temperament.

It can create fanatics by taking your mind intense into things. It is temporary happiness (fire consumes itself fast unless there are many resources), And of course star 9 can cause a place catching fire when it meets bad flying stars.

Flying Stars for the month

Except the Flying stars for the year, there are also Flying Stars for each month separately. This means that each direction (South, SW, West etc) is occupied by a Flying Star during a specific month.

Chinese months do not start on the 1st of each month like we do in the West, as the Flying stars are based on the chinese solar calendar,
A new month is starting between the 4th and the 8th of a month.
For example, February is the month of the tiger and in 2025 it is starting the 3rd of February 2025 and not the 1st of February 2025.

Each month has a month flying star at each direction. When the month finishes, the old month star goes to some other direction and a new month star comes instead in its place. So each direction is influenced by the year Flying Star and the month Flying Star. Just for you info, there are day Flying stars and hour Flying stars. The month Flying Stars are considered weaker than the big energy of the year Flying Stars. They are triggering events. Its like having a bomb at a location during the whole year, but when the month comes someones triggers it and makes it explode. The year is like the host and the month is like the guest.

A Feng Shui consultant will usually mark on your floor plan what Flying Stars occupy each direction of your house or business. This is the original Flying Star chart of your space, which does not change, it is like the birthday "astrology" chart that remains the same. Year and month energies are similar to the transits of western astrology. The original chart is there, but things happen when year and month Flying Stars gang up to make things happen. For someone who is novice, it is impossible to know how to handle a group of Flying Star numbers. However I decided to write this book having in mind that I would like to help everyone to improve his,her life to the maximum possible. Even if you don't hire a professional Feng Shui consultant, you can still do things on your own and still be very correct. This is why, when you deal with month stars, I prefer that you play it safe and you reduce the effect of the bad flying stars only, especially star 5, if possible do stars 7 and 3. The rest of the Flying stars, its up to you if you want to try them out.

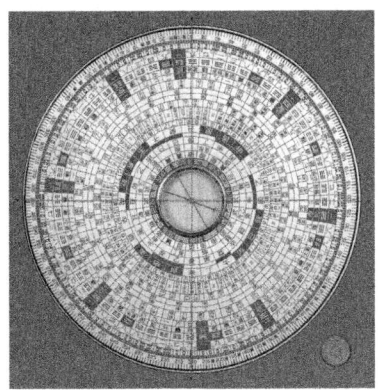

The Luo Pan compass

The Flying Star remedies for the monthly stars are exactly the same with the remedies for the year stars. For example, to reduce flying star 5 put a water salt therapy, do not stir it up with activity, do not face it etc.
Read carefully about the qualities of the 9 Flying Stars and how to deal with them at pages 8-29.

You treat the year Flying Stars by using the remedies I already mentioned in this book, these remedies stay there for the whole year. Once the year has expired, then you move the remedies to the location of the year star that you want to treat. Then you prepare another set of remedies for treating the month, each month you put each remedy at the location of the month star that you want to treat.

Below you will find the month flying stars for the year. For easy reference, at the same table you have the flying star of the year. So you can both year and month stars together at the same direction. The star on the left is the year flying star, the star on the right is the month flying star.

The year of the wood snake
03.02.2025-03.02.2026

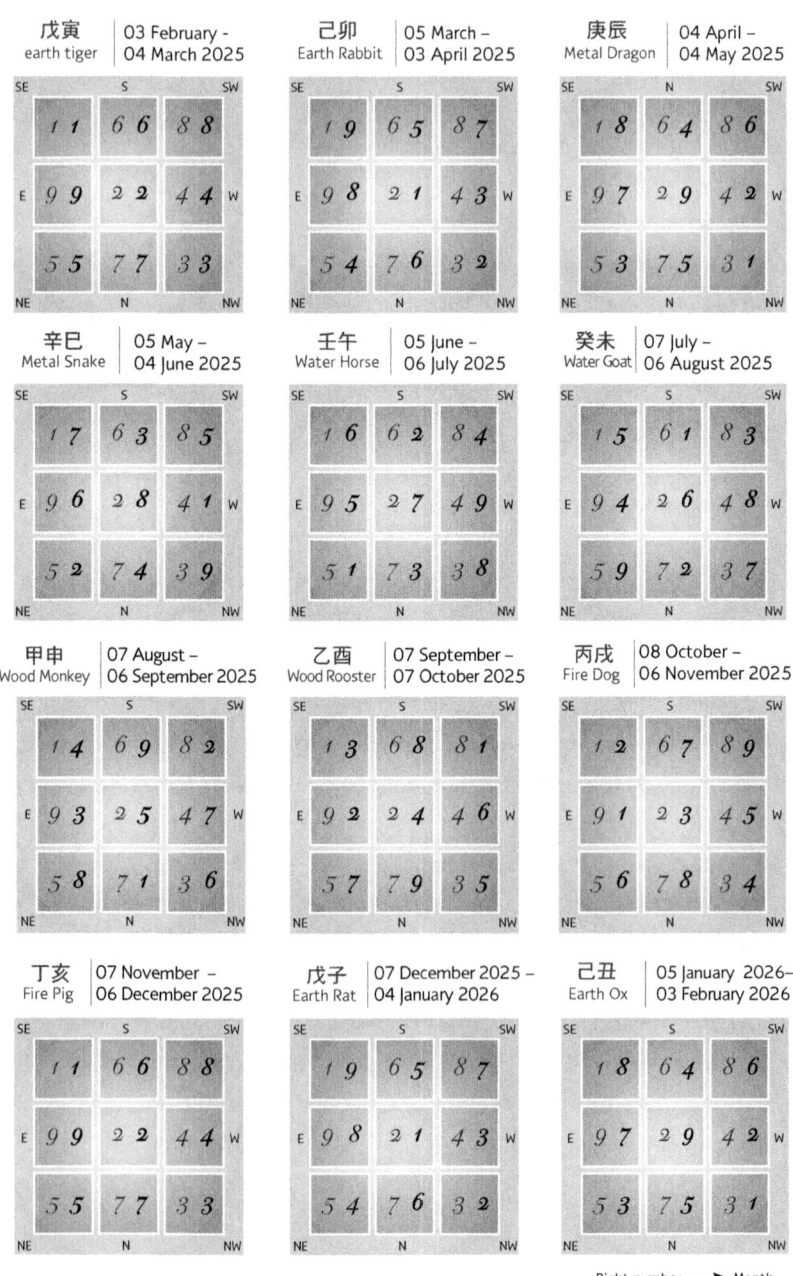

Right number → Month
Left number → Year

Grand Duke in SE 3

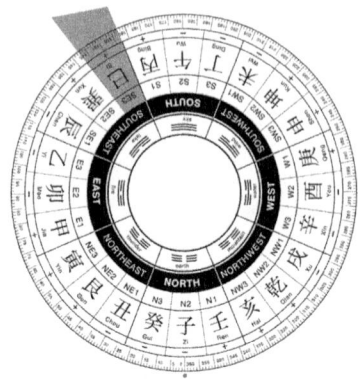

The Grand Duke is also known with the name Tai Sui. He is the highest force of the year, he is the boss of the year.

There is a famous chinese saying "there is nothing better than working with the Grand Duke, there is nothing worse than going against him". If you make him happy he will help you, if you go against him he will create serious trouble.

The Grand Duke is actually the position of the shadow of planet Jupiter on planet earth, and Jupiter is the biggest planet of our solar system. His magnetic influence on us is huge.

He is occupying only 15 degrees of the compass, every year the Grand Duke is changing position, these 15 degrees are the same like the chinese animal of the specific year. For example, in the year of the ox the Grand Duke is occupying the direction of the ox in the Feng Shui compass, in the year of the tiger the Grand Duke is occupying the direction of the Tiger and so on.

> **The Grand Duke in 2025 is located in the SE 3**

There is another famous chinese saying: "You can sit on the Grand Duke but you cannot face him". The force of Grand Duke can be so negative, it can even kill you. Its effects will usually happen in the same year but it can extend to up to 3 years.

The old times the chinese generals in order to win the battle, they were using the help of the Grand Duke. They would attack the enemy by having the direction of the Grand Duke at their back. For example if the Grand Duke was in the North, they would attack towards the South, ensuring their back is at the North.

A famous modern example of going against the Grand Duke is the battle of Waterloo. It was the year of the pig in 1815, when the Grand Duke was located at the pig direction (Northwest), Napoleon marched with his army towards the Northwest and against the Grand Duke. He was defeated.

How to avoid the Grand Duke:
• Do not dig (move earth), do not construct or decorate, do not hit a nail in a wall, do not cut trees at the location of the Grand Duke
• Do not face him, do not travel against him, do not more house by going against him
• Don't face him when you are on your bed
• Do not make constructions at your building if the entrance of the building is at the location of the Grand Duke
• Do not renovate, do not construct a building if the facing of the building is same as the Grand Duke

If you must make renovations there, read the sector of this book "renovation

& construction" because you need to choose auspicious dates and do some other tricks as well.

If you must make an important trip or move house towards the direction of the Grand Duke, you may do a trick. Go to another direction frist, sleep there, and the next day you go to your final destination. This way you avoid to travel towards the Grand Duke.

If your Chinese animal (based on your year of birth) is clashing the Grand Duke, do not travel against the Grand Duke.

If your Chinese animal (based on your year of birth) is clashing the Grand Duke, do not travel the month that clashes the Grand Duke.

In 2025, the year of the snake, do not travel towards the direction of the snake (SE 3), especially if you are born in the year of the pig, and especially avoid it during the month of the pig (November).

The usual Feng Shui remedies to deal with the Grand Duke are:
• Place a dragon-head turtle facing the Grand Duke.
• Put a talisman at the Grand Duke location of your house or business. Once the year is gone, you need to burn the talisman. The talisman for this year comes together with this book.
• If you are born in the same year like

Dragon-head turtle

the Grand Duke, keep the talisman with you at all times during that year. For example, if you are born in the year of the snake, you need to have with you, during the year of the snake, the talisman for the snake year.

• If you are born in the year opposite to the Grand Duke, keep a talisman with you as well. For example, if you are born in the year in pig, you are clashing (fighting) the Grand Duke.

Many people are happy when the current year is the same with their year of birth, they think it is going to be their year and everything is going to be fantastic.

Actually this is not true. If your year of birth is same with the Grand Duke, you are offending the Grand Duke (its like as you dare to sit on his neck!). And this is bad, because you are facing him, your year of birth goes against him!

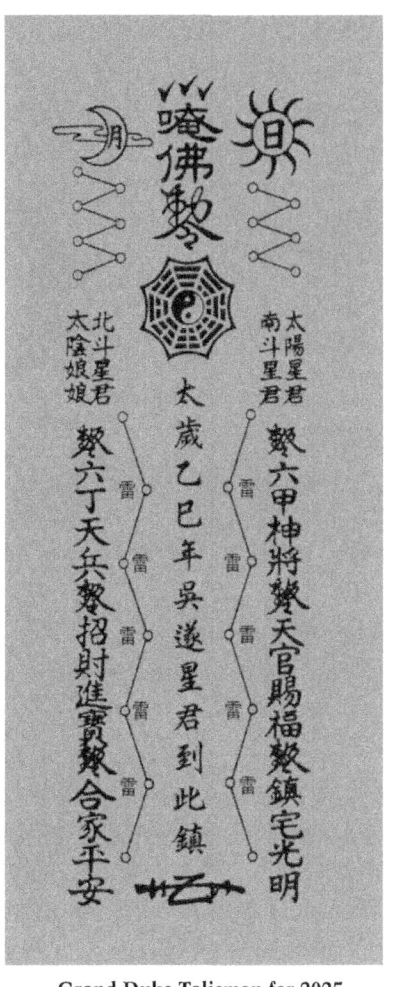

Grand Duke Talisman for 2025

If you are born in the year of the snake, you are offending the Grand Duke. Carry the talisman for the Grand Duke and carry a monkey pendant at all times.

Clash in the direction of the pig = NW 3

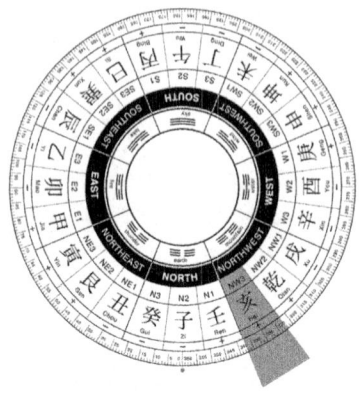

Clash is also known as Sui Po or Year Breaker. It brings money loss.

Clash is the animal (sector on the Feng Shui compass) that is opposite to the animal of the year. The animal that clashes the year, is fighting against the year, the year is the biggest and strongest energy.

> **"You may face against the Clash, but you cannot sit on the Clash".**

The sector of a house or business that is clashing the energy of the year is not stable, it gets consumed. If the door of your house is inside that Clash sector, it it easy to spend a lot of money, its more easy to spend it than to earn it. Clash is always a bad energy, while the Grand Duke that can be also good and bad, as I explained before. But when the Grand Duke is bad, he is much worse than the Clash.

> **Clash in 2025 is located in NW 3.**

What to do to deal with Clash:
- Avoid construction, renovation, digging or moving earth by any means at the location of Clash.
- Avoid construction, renovation, digging or moving earth if the building is sitting at Clash.
- Avoid sitting with your back towards Clash.

If you dig or sit at Clash, you will lose money in the same year. Choose auspicious dates and do some other tricks as explained in the chapter of this book about renovations. If you really have to do renovations there, try not to be present during the renovation works. If you think about it, when you sit having your back at Clash, you have to face the Grand Duke, which is bad. By activating clash this way it is like going against the Grand Duke.

3 Shars in the South

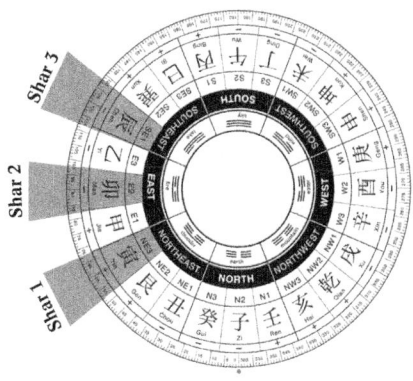

The 3 Shars are also known as 3 Killings.
3 Shars is three areas of the Feng Shui compass that have negative effect. Its like backstabbbing. Each area covers 15 degrees. The worse Shar is the middle one, which is always a cardinal direction.

In 2025 the 3 shars are located NE 3, E 2, SE 1.

The calculation of the 3 Shars is based on a 4 pillars of destiny formula, actually many Chinese astrology formulas have application in Feng Shui. There are year 3 Shar (calculation based on year), month 3 Shar (calculation based on month), there is even 3 Shar of the day and hour. The day and hour 3 Shar influence is not strong.

Here is the effect of each of the 3 Shars:
- The first Shar creates robbery, loss of money and is often related to travel (its always a travel horse direction)
- The second Shar creates injury, illness, sex problems or excessive sex (its always a peach blossom direction)
- The third Shar creates delays, obstacles, being stuck, loneliness (its always an earth grave direction). It is less serious than the other shars.

What to do to deal with the 3 Shars of the year:
- Do not sit while you have your back against the 3 shars (bed, office etc). Turn your bed or chair to avoid any shar.
- Avoid digging, construction, renovation, planting tree, at the location of any of the shars. Especially do not begin construction from there.
- Do not have your building sitting on the Shar of the year.
- Place 3 Qi Lin, one Qi Lin at each Shar location, facing outside towards each Shar. Alternatively place at the central Shar a pot with a cheap plant because it will get sick and absorb this energy.

Qi Lin

Earth Shar in NE 3 and E 2

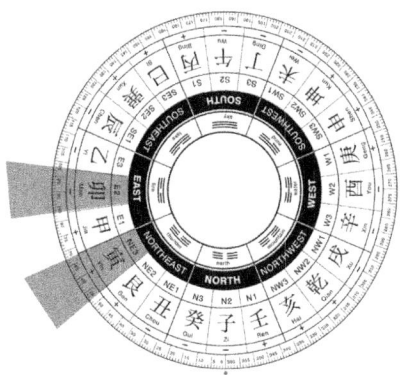

Earth Shar are two sectors of the compass also known as Wu Du Tian & Ji Du Tian. They are calculated based on the heavenly stem of the year. Each Earth Shar covers 15 degrees of the Feng Shui compass and you are not supposed to disturb them by renovations, constructions etc.

> **In 2025 Wu Du TIan is in the direction of the tiger (NE 3), Ji Du Tian is in the direction of the rabbit (E 2). For some masters, in 2025 Wu Du Tian is also the direction of the rat (N 2) and the Ji Du Tian is also the direction of the ox (NE 1).**

If you are planning to do renovations, it is wise to avoid renovations in the day that is the same with the Earth shar. If you observe nature, not even the swallows avoid constructing their nest during the Earth Shar days. You may find the Earth Shar days in the Tong Shu section of this book, it is all the horse and goat days of the year. You easily find in the Tong Shu what is the animal of the day,It is inside the box that contains date number (21, 23, 24 March etc) the day name (Monday, Tuesday etc).
This way you will know what days not to construct.

> **In 2025 avoid renovations & constructions in the day of the tiger and the rabbit.**

Flying Grand Duke in the West

The Flying Grand Duke is also know as Hidden Construction Shar, it is another energy that we need to take into consideration in Feng Shui. It brings money loss and illness. Avoid construction, renovation, planting tree.

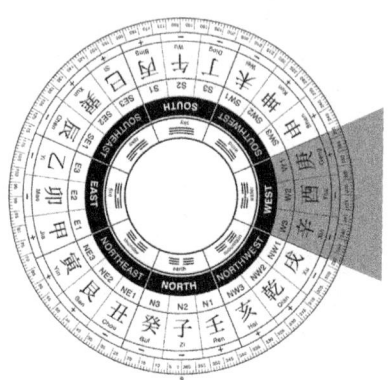

In 2025 the Flying Grand Duke is in the West.

If in a specific year the Flying Grand Duke happens to be in the center, no construction at all should be done that year.
For those we appreciate knowledge, I am offering the formula openly.
This is how you calculate the formula of the Flying Grand Duke, i give you as example the year 2025.
1. Find the location of the Grand Duke. In 2025 Grand Duke is SE 3.
2. Find the flying star that is located at the sector of the Grand Duke in the original Lo Shu. For example in 2025, the Grand Duke is in SE 3, in the original Lo Shu we have 4 in the SE.
3. Put the ruling flying star of the specific year in the middle and fly it.
    E.g. in 2025 it is the 2 is in the middle.

4. Find what direction this number is occupying at step two. This is the location of the Flying Grand Duke. E.g. in the grid which has 2 in the center, we look for star 4 of step two, 4 is in the West. In 2025 the Flying Grand Duke is in the West.

Li Shih in the SW 2

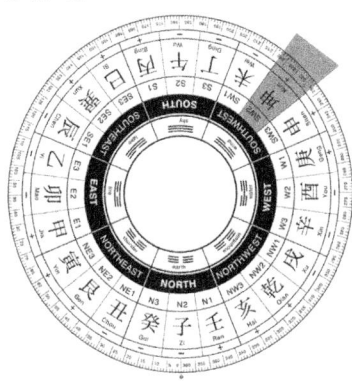

> In 2025 Li Shih is in the SW 2.

This is the "bodyguard" of the emperor. If you irritate it, it will give you a very strong punch.

It covers 15 degrees in the Feng Shui compass. Avoid construction, digging, renovation, plant tree etc.

If Li Shih is located in the same sector with the annual Flying Star 5, it is extremely inauspicious if you dig earth.

If you really need to make construction there, read the section of this book about renovations.

You may also put there a set of coins of the 9 emperors, or place a mini Lo Shu compass to face it. Personally I am not into using objects to reduce this kind of construction shars, I prefer not to disturb them at all.

2025
where to avoid construction in the year

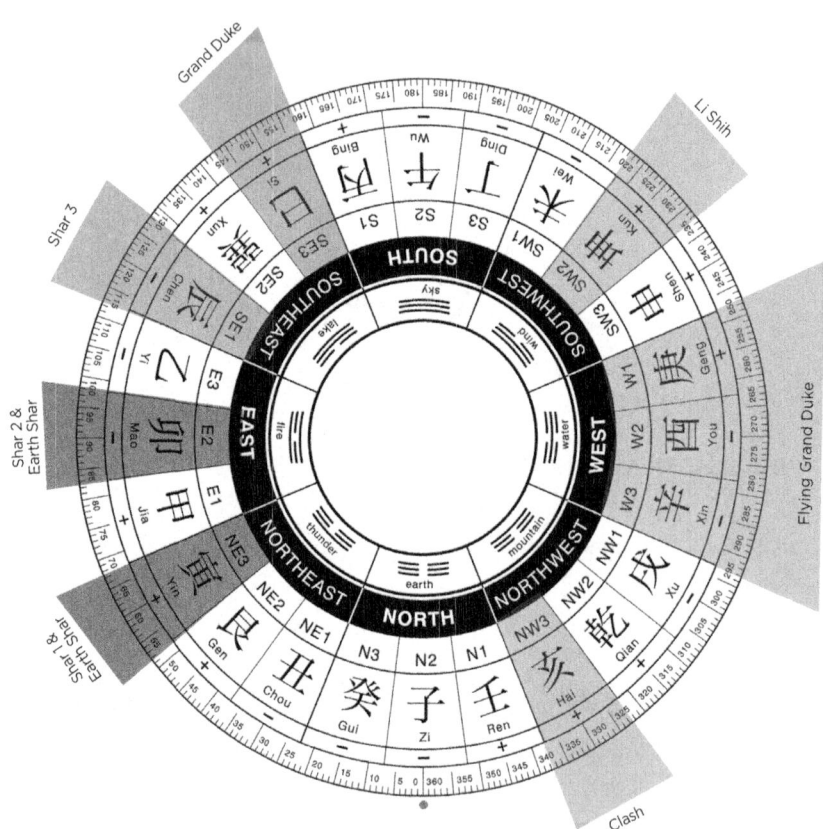

The worse of all is: Flying Star 5, Grand Duke, 3 Shars, Clash

Renovation & construction
where to avoid construction each month
Flying star 5 & 3 shar of the month

February
03.02.2025 - 04.03.2025

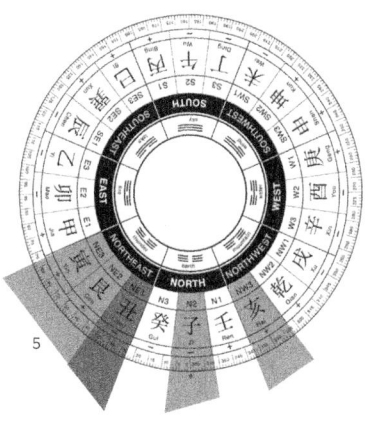

March
05.03.2025 - 03.04.2025

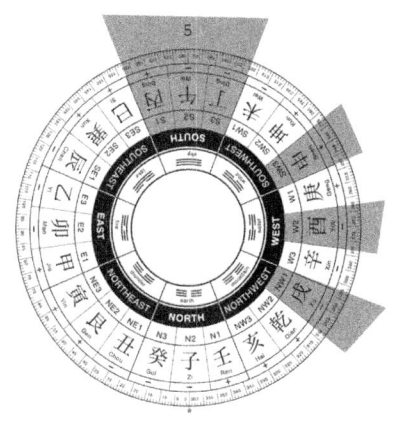

April
04.04.2025 - 04.05.2025

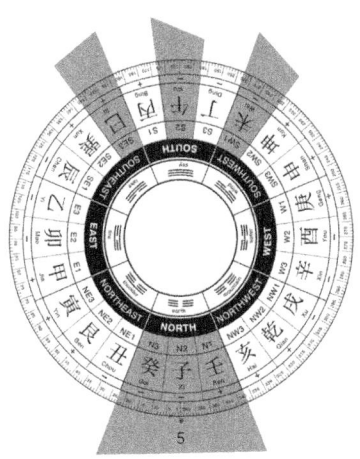

May
05.05.2025 - 04.06.2025

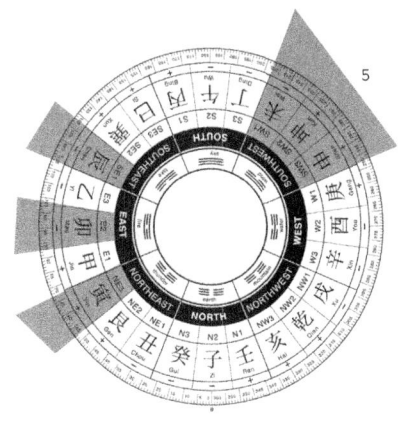

Renovation & construction
where to avoid construction each month

Flying star 5 & 3 shar of the month

June
05.06.2025 - 06.07.2025

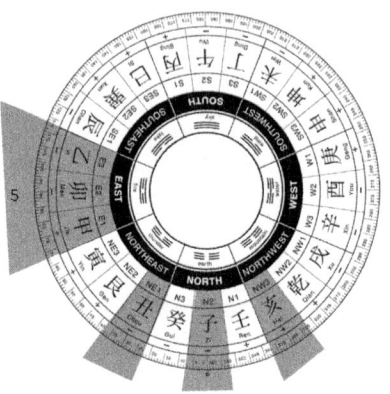

July
07.07.2025 - 06.08.2025

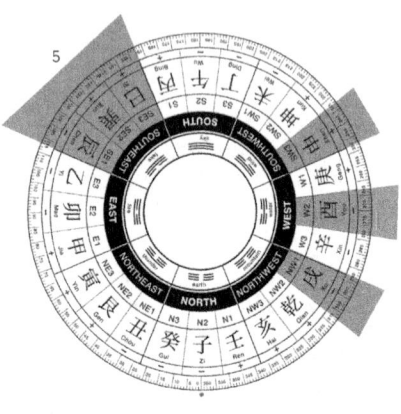

August
07.08.2025 - 06.09.2025

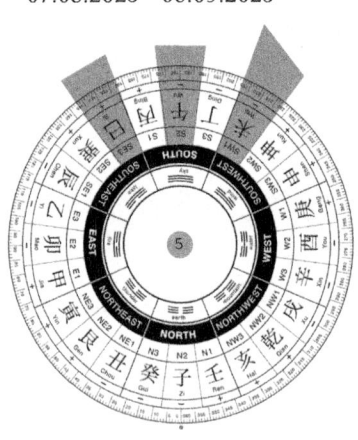

September
07.09.2025 - 07.10.2025

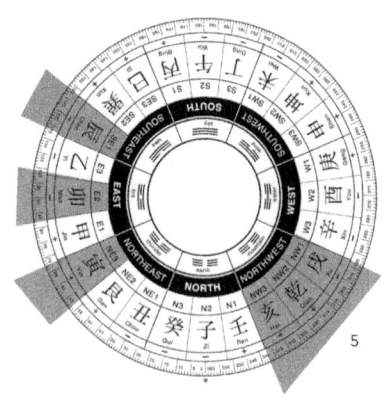

Renovation & construction
where to avoid construction each month

Flying star 5 & 3 shar of the month

October
08.10.2025 - 06.11.2025

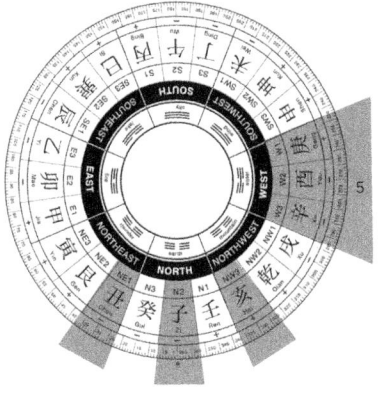

November
07.11.2025 - 06.12.2025

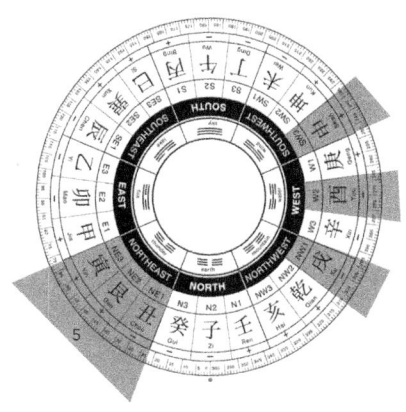

December
07.12.2025 - 04.01.2026

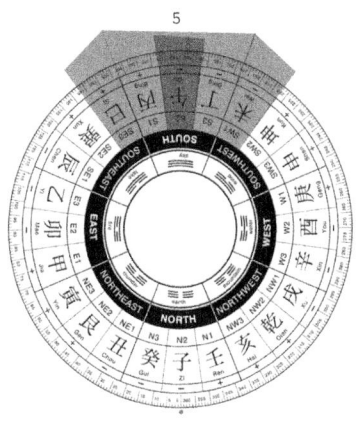

January
05.01.2026 - 03.02.2026

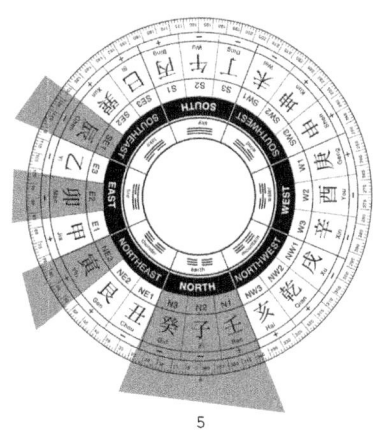

Renovation & construction
where to avoid construction each day

Do not renovate, construct, move earth at a location with the daily flying star 5. You may find the location of the daily flying star 5 at page 96.
Also do not renovate, construct, move earth at the location which has 3 shars relationship with the day:
- The day of the monkey, rat, dragon, do not dig at the location of the snake (SE3), horse (S2), goat (SW1).
- The day of the tiger, horse, dog, do not dig at the location of the pig (NW3), rat (N2), ox (NE1).
- The day of the pig, rabbit, goat, do not dig at the location of the monkey (SW3), rooster (W2), dog (NW1).
- The day of the snake, rooster, ox, do not dig at the location of the tiger (NE3), rabbit (E2), dragon (SE1).

You may find the exact location of these directions at the end of this book, find the diagram with the 24 mountains of the chinese compass.

Renovation & construction
where and when to start construction

Sometimes you must construct or dig earth, although there are sectors with bad energy. There are some ways to deal with such problems, such as:
- The Great Sun Formula
- The 3 white stars (1, 6, 8 white) & the 4 construction auspicious stars (Great Yin, Great Yang, Dragon Virtue, Fortune Virtue)

The Great Sun Formula gives you 4 periods of time during one year, each period lasts around 14 days. During these days, the sun is shining at the back of your house, so nothing bad can happen. So, you may renovate during that period. However, if you have the choice not to renovate that year, do not do it. The formulas I will show you should be applied when you have no choice. These formulas are like Feng Shui remedies, they improve things but cannot make the bad energies totally disappear, things can still happen but with less force.

It is not easy for the novice Feng Shui person to apply the Great Sun Formula, as it is necessary to use a Feng Shui compass (the Feng Shui compass is also known as Luo Pan compass). You need to take an exact measurement of the back of the building. You may know the back of the building if you had a Feng Shui consultation. If you are not sure of your measurement, do not use this formula.

When you read below the formula and I say "8 August plus 14 days", I mean you may construct any time between the 8th of August and all the period until maximum 14 days later.

Great Sun Formula

If the back of your house is South 1, construct: 3 February plus 14 days, 4 April plus 14 days, 7 August plus 14 days, 7 December plus 14 days.

If the back of your house is South 2, construct: 20 January plus 14 days, 20 March plus 14 days, 22 July plus 14 days, 22 November plus 14 days.

If the back of your house is South 3, construct: 5 January plus 14 days, 5 March plus 14 days, 7 July plus 14 days, 11 November plus 14 days.

If the back of your house is SW 1, construct: 18 February plus 14 days, 21 June plus 14 days, 23 October plus 14 days, 21 December plus 14 days.

If the back of your house is SW 2, construct: 3 February plus 14 days, 5 June plus 14 days, 8 October plus 14 days, 7 December plus 14 days.

If the back of your house is SW 3, construct: 20 January plus 14 days, 21 May plus 14 days, 23 September plus 14 days, 22 November plus 14 days.

If the back of your house is West 1, construct: 5 January plus 14 days, 5 May plus 14 days, 7 September plus 14 days, 9 November plus 14 days.

If the back of your house is West 2, construct: 20 April plus 14 days, 23 August plus 14 days, 23 October plus 14 days, 21 December plus 14 days.

If the back of your house is West 3, construct: 4 April plus 14 days, 7 August plus 14 days, 8 October plus 14 days, 7 December plus 14 days.

If the back of your house is NW 1, construct: 20 March plus 14 days, 22 July plus 14 days, 23 September plus 14 days, 22 November plus 14 days.

If the back of your house is NW 2, construct: 5 March plus 14 days, 7 July plus 14 days, 8 September plus 14 days, 7 November plus 14 days.

If the back of your house is NW 3, construct: 18 February plus 14 days, 22 July plus 14 days, 23 August plus 14 days, 23 October plus 14 days.

If the back of your house is North 1, construct: 3 February plus 14 days, 7 July plus 14 days, 7 August plus 14 days, 8 October plus 14 days.

If the back of your house is North 2, construct: 20 January plus 14 days, 21 May plus 14 days, 22 July plus 14 days, 23 September plus 14 days.

If the back of your house is North 3, construct: 5 January plus 14 days, 5 May plus 14 days, 22 July plus 14 days, 7 September plus 14 days.

If the back of your house is NE 1, construct: 20 April plus 14 days, 7 July plus 14 days, 23 August plus 14 days, 21 December plus 14 days.

If the back of your house is NE 2, construct: 4 April plus 14 days, 4 April plus 14 days, 7 June plus 14 days, 7 December plus 14 days.

If the back of your house is NE 3, construct: 20 March plus 14 days, 21 May plus 14 days, 22 July plus 14 days, 22 November plus 14 days.

If the back of your house is East 1, construct: 5 March plus 14 days, 5 May plus 14 days, 7 July plus 14 days, 7 November plus 14 days.

If the back of your house is East 2, construct: 18 February plus 14 days, 20 April plus 14 days, 21 June plus 14 days, 23 October plus 14 days.

If the back of your house is East 3, construct: 3 February plus 14 days, 4 April plus 14 days, 5 June plus 14 days, 8 October plus 14 days.

If the back of your house is SE 1, construct: 20 January plus 14 days, 20 March plus 14 days, 21 May plus 14 days, 23 September plus 14 days.

If the back of your house is SE 2, construct: 5 January plus 14 days, 5 March plus 14 days, 5 May plus 14 days, 7 September plus 14 days.

If the back of your house is SE 3, construct: 18 February plus 14 days, 20 April plus 14 days, 23 August plus 14 days, 21 December plus 14 days.

Important note: The above mentioned starting dates may vary, so it is better to avoid the first and the last day of the 15 day period.

The 3 white stars & the 4 auspicious construction stars

Here we use 2 formulas together at the same time if possible, or at least one of them. When using these two formulas we can even dig and make construction at the location of the Grand Duke, they may even help you with construction inside the Clash sector.

First formula is that we use any of the 3 white stars (1 white, 6 white and 8 white) and especially the auspicious during Age 8 flying 1 and 8, so find the direction they occupy in the flying star grid of any given year.

Second formula is that we use the 4 auspicious constructions stars called Tai Yin (Great Yin), Tai Yang (Great Yang), Fude (Fortune Virtue), Longde (Dragon Virtue). These stars can protect you from the Grand Duke and even the Clash as they are calculated based on the Grand Duke.
The 4 construction stars occupy 15 degrees each.

In 2025:
- Great Yang is in the Horse (S2)
- Great Yin is in the Monkey (SW3)
- Dragon Virtue is in the Rat (N2)
- Fortune Virtue is in the Tiger (NE3).

This is how we prioritize the selection of where to construct even when there are negative influences:
1. The sector that has no negative influence (no annual 5, no shars, no Grand Duke, no clash etc) plus any of the annual white stars 6, 8, 1 (we prefer 1) plus any of the 4 construction stars.
2. The sector that has no negative influence, plus any of the 4 construction stars. Or a sector that has no negative influence plus any of the annual white stars 6, 8, 1.
3. The sector with negative influence plus any of the 4 construction stars.
4. The sector with negative influence plus annual white star 6, 8, 1.
5. The sector with negative influence without any white star, without any auspicious construction star.

And here is the conclusion, ready calculated for you:

> **Where to start construction in 2025:**
> **There are these possibilities:**
> 1. SW3: no negative influence plus annual 8, plus great yin
> 2. S2: No negative influence, plus annual 6, plus great yang
> 3. S1 & S3: no negative influence plus annual 6
> 4. SW1: no negative influence plus annual 8
> 5. SE2: no negative influence plus annual 1
> 6. E1 & E3: no negative influence plus annual 9

2025
Negative and positive influences for construction

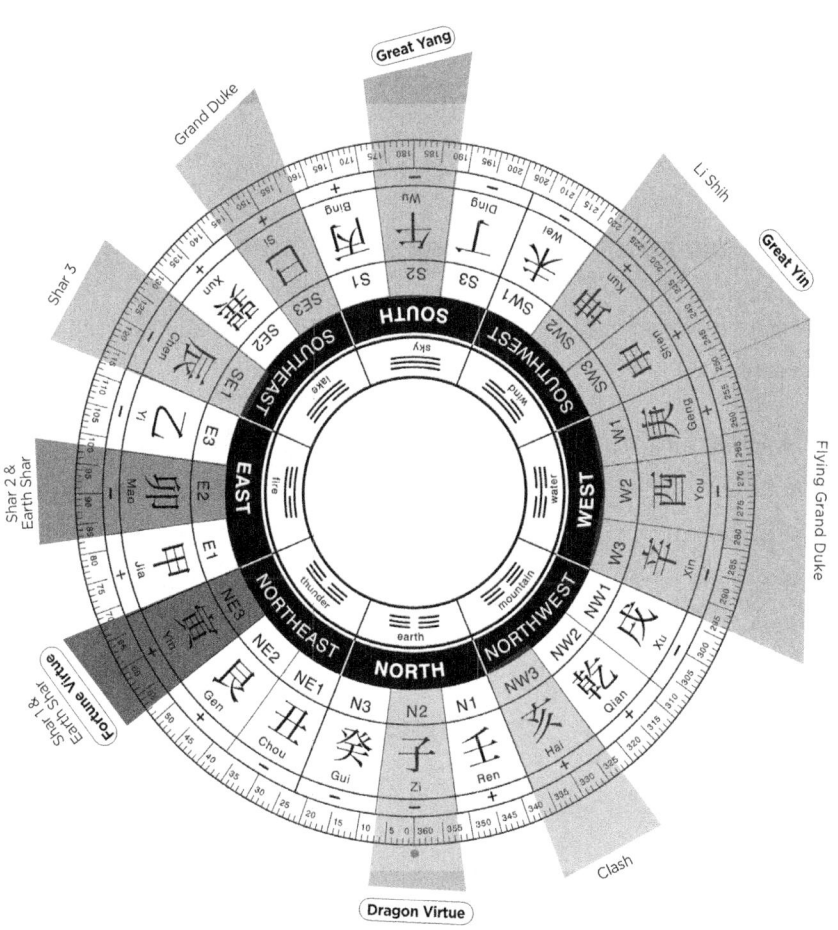

Choosing the right day to start construction

- Avoid the day that clashes with you. Go to the Tong Shu section, sector "clash" avoid to see your chinese animal sign.
- Avoid days that clash with the year and month, avoid days that are in 3 shar relationship with the year or month. Go to the Tong Shu section, sector "Influence", avoid to see bombs with numbers 1, 2, 3 or 4 respectively.
- Avoid days that the Tong Shu describes as bad for construction at sector "Bad".

Days and hours to avoid Feng Shui consultation

There are certain days and hours that one should not do any Feng Shui consultation. They bring bad luck to the consultant.

04 January 2025	26 April 2025	28 August 2025
05 January 2025	09 May 2025	10 September 2025
17 January 2025	21 May 2025	22 September 2025
29 January 2025	02 June 2025	04 October 2025
11 February 2025	15 June 2025	12 October 2025
14 February 2025	16 June 2025	17 October 2025
23 February 2025	27 June 2025	29 October 2025
08 March 2025	10 July 2025	11 November 2025
20 March 2025	22 July 2025	23 November 2025
01 April 2025	03 August 2025	05 December 2025
14 April 2025	13 August 2025	11 December 2025
15 April 2025	16 August 2025	18 December 2025
		30 December 2025

If you want to take it into a step further, you may also avoid to do Feng Shui consultation during certain hours. Here it is:

- The day of the rat, avoid ox (01.00- 02.59) and horse (11.00-12.59) hours.
- The day of the ox avoid snake (09.00-10.59) and pig (21.00-22.59) hours.
- The day of the tiger, avoid tiger (03.00-04.59) and horse (11.00-12.59) hours.
- The day of the rabbit, avoid dragon (07.00-08.59) and dog (19.00-20.59) hours.
- The day of the dragon, avoid snake (09.00-10.59) and ox (01.00-02.59) hours.
- The day of the snake, avoid dragon (07.00-08.59) and dog (19.00-20.59) hours.
- The day of the horse, avoid rabbit (05.00-06.59) and monkey(15.00-16.59) hours.
- The day of the goat, avoid horse (11.00-12.59) and dragon (07.00-08.59) hours.
- The day of the monkey, avoid dog (19.00-20.59) and ox (01.00-02.59) hours.
- The day of the rooster, avoid rat (23.00-00.59) and horse (11.00-12.59) hours.
- The day of the dog, avoid rabbit (05.00-06.59) and horse (11.00-12.59) hours.
- The day of the pig, avoid dragon (07.00-08.59 and rabbit (05.00-06.59) hours.

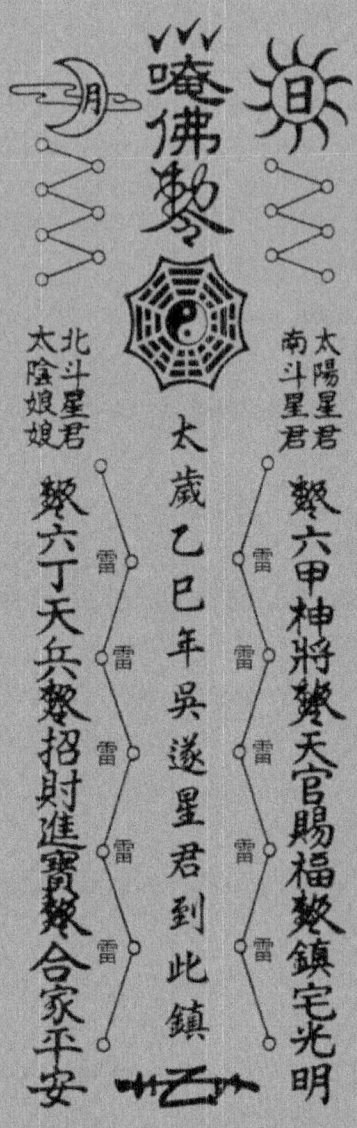

Grand Duke Talisman 2025

- Place the talisman in the Southeast (sector 3) of your home or business.

- If you have a snake or pig in your chart, carry this talisman until 3 February 2026.

4 Pillars of destiny
2025

World predictions 2025

The year of the wood snake (03 February 2025-03 February 2026)

According to the Chinese Astrology system called 4 Pillars of Destiny (also known as Bazi or 8 characters), 2025 is the year of wood snake and it lasts from 3rd February 2025 until 3rd February 2026.

This information is found in the Chinese Calendar, a book that converts any given date into the 5 elements and the 12 Chinese Animals. According to this system, any given year can be described with an element and a Chinese animal.

Chinese used to write on bamboo from top to bottom.
The year 2025 is described by yin wood at the top and snake at the bottom. Snake belongs to yin fire element and inside it hides yang metal, yang fire and yang earth. This is the way it looks;

In order to make predictions for 2025:
1. We analyze the qualities of yin wood, yin fire, snake and all those combined together.
2. As Chinese writing is like pictures, we also visualize the picture by putting together the yin wood with the yin fire snake.

3. We use Symbolic Stars and we find out which Symbolic stars are valid in 2025.
4. We consider the hidden elements hiding inside the snake (yang metal, yang fire, yang earth).
5. We check what happened 60 years ago, or even 120 years ago, as this was also the year of wood snake.

Society & politics

Yin wood is a small plant like a flower, a climbing ivy, the grass and the fern. Yin wood is flexible and adaptive. Think how a small plant will find its way to the sun by finding the most incredible ways to survive.

Yin wood is not like yang wood. While yang wood is the leader, yin wood is the number two, it is the advisor to the leader. Yin wood people are the strategists behind the scenes.! Such people will be showing up in 2025, they will become apparent.

Yin wood is **diplomatic** and **tactful**. Likewise, 2025 will also make the people wanting to find their way to a better tomorrow by negotiating, by diplomacy, by being tactful. Yin wood is a very **sweet talker**, so in 2025 we will hear a lot of nice and soft words. The months that wood is strong, we might even see **peace agreements** and **ceasefire** between countries, or at least negotiations and efforts for finding solutions through diplomacy.

This explains why 60 years ago, in 1964 some countries gained independence after diplomacy, such as Singapore, Maldives and Gambia. Also the war between India and Pakistan over Kashmir leaded to ceasefire. So there is a chance for peace at some parts of the world in 2025, there will be definitely **efforts to resolve international conflicts.** This could lead to potential peace agreement between Russia and NATO.

However, bear in mind that small plants **do not stay firm in their opinion,** they **adapt** and **bend** where the wind goes in order to survive, so this peace "love" might not last. Ukraine war started in tiger year and might come to an end after 3 years in the end of spring "season".
Maybe some countries will manage to get some peace during the yin wood period of time during 2025. Yin wood is willing to compromise in order to achieve long lasting success, as it always wants results to last.

Countries will be very adaptive about their opinions in 2025. A typical yin wood trait is that when its existence is under thread, the best way for yin wood to reach the sun is to step on a big tree or a bigger plant to hold itself. So in 2025 I expect **country alliances** to become priority in politics. Yin wood appreciates the help of others in order to get what it wants.

However, this peace seeking energy is very **volatile** and easy to change, this is for **three** reasons.
First, because yin wood is sitting on yin fire, this is the image of a flower, this makes the flower hot. It is the image of a **withered flower,** a flower without energy. So the diplomatic talks are exhausted and weak during some months of 2025.
Second, because of the presence of yin fire (snake) in the year 2025. Yin fire is like candle fire.

Candle fire is unpredictable and emotional. We all know that we should never let candle fire unattended because it can suddenly burn everything down. Snake is a part of the so called "fire penalty" in Chinese astrology, causing **fire disasters.**

Third, snake is an animal that acts like a **chameleon** and it is very **unpredictable.** This is why I do not expect 2025 to be a peaceful year.

Also 60 years ago, it was also a yin wood snake year, there was war in Vietnam. There was also war in Kashmir between Pakistan and India.

So, this phenomenal mood to find a diplomatic solution and stop fighting can be easily jeopardized because of yin fire, making people having an explosive mood and making war.

Yin fire is very emotional, one moment its quiet, and the other moment it can kill you. Yin fire is also **explosive fire,** it is **fire arms**, bullets and **bombs.** The snake is hiding yang fire in it, yang fire is **nuclear energy** too. Nuclear disaster, either through dirty bombs or real nuclear ones might be in our attention and might even become reality.

The yin fire related explosive mood will create **hot temper, riots** and **protests** in 2025.
Military coups are possible as well, as a coup is also a kind of riot. Also inside the snake there is the hidden element of yang metal, yang metal is the big sword of the army.

The snake is an animal that moves on the ground and it is cold blooded. In I Ching divination (King Wen style) we related the snake to **hidden/strange matters, ghosts** and the **dead.** I would not be surprised if in 2025 we have this kind of events too. We will see strange things happening, **increased deaths, assassinations.**

60 years ago, Ku Klux Klan (a hidden political group) was still around and active. Also chemical warfare against Vietkong was confirmed (chemical war is invisible and nusty like a snake).

Yin wood is the neck of the human body, as it shows up in the heavenly stem of the year, it is easy to attract energies to chop it off. Yin wood attracts its opposite energy which is yin metal, yin metal is the dagger, the small knife and it is very **revengeful** energy.

The snake is fond of **scandals**. We will even see more news about ghosts and the **metaphysical** world.

It is also known that a snake will ride others in order to get to the top of society. Nobody trusts a snake, because it can do double dealings. This could affect 2025 by making some **country leaders playing it double in diplomatic fairs.**

On the other hand, snake is known that likes **detective** work and has a **talent for research.** Let us see what the snake will discover in 2025.

Yin fire (snake) is about energy and electricity. Yin fire is the lamp pole. There can be sudden **problems of electricity** and **electronics** in 2025. 60 years ago, also a wood snake year, there was an electricity blackout where 30 million people in New York were left without power for 13 hours.

As our society is depending heavily in electronics, any blackout happening today brings serious chaos affecting not only buildings but also banking and transportations.

Also remember the **detective** talent of the snake, it will be present in 2025. About the general mood of the 2025 I expect that it will be quite controversial.

Yin wood has **no confidence,** it is not standing up, it has no punch, it prefers to be diplomatic. Yin wood has no endurance, but it is **possessive.** Think how much of the earth is occupied by grass, we don't even realize how silently yin wood has taken our planet, it loves to expand. The love for expansion of yin wood will mark the politics of 2025, leaders will try to expand their actual territory or territory of influence (by climbing on stronger "tree", aka stronger countries or unions and making coalitions).

On the other hand, yin fire is about **acting in an emotional way** (candle fire) and it can suddenly be very explosive. Yin fire is really unpredictable, and in this article I am trying to make exact predictions looking at all parameters. We will see things happening in this frame, we humans have the choice to follow this narrative or a much better version of it. What is the better version?

Let me also give you some good news as well about the coming year 2025.

The snake is an animal related to **renewal** and **transformation.** We all know that the snake is shedding its old skin and transforms itself afresh.

60 years ago, many new countries were being born from the decayed bones of empires (e.g. Zimbabwe). Also 2025 will be a year of rebirth (after death).

We reach a moment in society that it is time to change and transform. We are going to make a new beginning in 2025. Snake is related to **spirituality,** it is the energy kundalini, it is the guardian of the treasure of Indiana Jones films.

We are going to leave the old thinking. Fire element is about the eyes, it is about seeing. It is our third eye as well, we can have **intuition** more than ever. As fire is hiding yang fire inside, yang fire is like the sun. There is no shadow under the strong sun, so no secret can hide under the light of the sun. I expect a lot of hidden secrets coming out in public.

For the first time after many years, we see fire element being present in 2025. Fire is about optimism and the feeling of happiness. Although snake is not reliable fire (candle fire is not reliable), however it is finally appearing. We will finally see the **light at the end of the tunnel.** We will see things under a new light. It is a new beginning.

In 2025 we see the first year of fire appearing, at the same time we see again fire element appearing during Period 9 (2024-2044). This makes the fire element even more prominent and important. We will see fire getting in full swing from year 2025 onwards.

I have a lot of key words about fire and Period 9 in my book "Feng Shui Trends for Period 9". You may get my book in Amazon.

Environment & weather

The year 2025 is about yin wood sitting on yin fire. Yin wood is related to the Wind trigram of the I Ching. Yin fire is related to energy. Putting the two words together, wind and energy, I get the word "wind energy".
Also yin fire (snake) is a long narrow object, it is like a candle. At the top end of the candle, you have something that looks like 3 huge petals or 3 huge leaves. What comes again in my mind is the wind turbines.

Wind turbine energy will be in focus during 2025. Are they good for the environment or not?

Yin wood is about the SE trigram of the I Ching, this trigram is also known as wind. Weather phenomenon related to winds will be very strong in 2025. **Tornados, storms, hurricanes** and similar phenomenon will happen more than usually.

Yin wood is directly related to small plants and agriculture. It is small sensitive wood. Yin wood appears as heavenly stem in the year 2025, so environment issues will be in focus. As yin wood is sitting on yin fire, this is clearly the image of a **withered small plant** because of **hot weather.**
Also in year 1965, another wood snake year, there was serious **crop failure** due to **draught** in many countries leading to starvation.

Yin wood is about the **environment,** so in 2025 we will focusing on how to protect the environment and the climate. **"Global warming"** will be in the center of attention, too.

I expect that **hot weather** due to fire snake in 2025 will cause problems with agriculture, leading to **skyrocketing prices of food.** Do not forget that plants is the food for animals too.

Snake belongs to fire element, specifically snake is yin fire and it has the same qualities like candle fire.

2025 is a wood fire year, wood is food to fire, meaning that fire element can be strong. Candle fire is dangerous explosive unpredictable fire. We might see volcano explosions, crops and **nature catching fire,** wood catching fire (e.g. forest fire).
Bomb explosions, nuclear explosions, even **building explosions** as an extension to general explosions happening around the planet. All happening **suddenly**, as yin fire has the quality of a suddenly changing situation.

We are in Period 9 (2024-2044) that is also fire element. Together with the wood fire year 2025, the weather will be extremely hot, especially during the summer months.

Health

As 2025 is about yin wood sitting on snake (yang fire), the human organs that will be more vulnerable in health problems will be directly related to these elements. Let us see what organs we need to pay attention this year.

Yin wood is the **neck, spine, fingers, nails, knee** and the **liver** & the **joints**.
Yin wood is small wood that is easy to break. Limbs.
Tendency for accidents involving the breaking of neck or joints.
Osteoporosis (dry wood) or inflammation of **small bones** will be an issue this year.
Yin wood also affects the **hair,** many people will lose their hair because the wood is too dry in this fire year. Dry **nails** that break.
In 2025 the **liver** will be hot because of the snake fire effect.
Motion problems such as Parkinsons because of wood.

Inflammation of the body, **circulation** & **heart** problems, **blood** problems, **vein thrombosis,** can be cause by the unexpected effect of yin fire snake. Yin fire also affects the nervous system, illness related to the **nerves** will be on the rise.

The snake in I Ching divination is related to mystery, death and spiritual things. It could be that in 2025 we see more **mysterious death** than usual.

60 years ago, also a wood snake year, death penalty was abolished for the first time before it became a law. So, being busy with death matters will be back.

Another organ that might suffer is metal. Yin wood as heavenly stem of 2025 may bring in the opposite energy which is metal. Metal is related to the **skin** and **lungs.** I am writing this article in August, and it has just been announced the Mpox as a new pandemic that just started in Africa.

Snake is considered the birth place of metal, so I consider that in 2025 we will see the birth of a new breathing/skin disease, so indeed in 2025 we will be facing **Mpox** as a health problem.

However, this metal is inside the fire, fire destroys the metal. Fire will destroy the metal and the skin of people, it will be like inflammation of the skin.

How bad is this new pandemic going to be? Not very bad., it will not be like Covid19.

When Covid19 appeared end of 2019, these were water and metal years. Water is about fear and metal is about depression.

From 2025 and for the coming next years, fire element is back, so people will not have fear. I don't expect that Mpox will have the same fear effect like Covid.

I also do not see massive wave of **vaccinations**. I don't think that people will go to vaccinated themselves like they did with Covid19. Because yin metal brings the vaccines and there is no yin metal in 2025, also the yang metal is very weak in 2025 (hiding under the snake). I hope my prediction will come true, I just observe data from the past and I inform you about what is likely to happen while just knowing the current news.

Economy & banking

The first half of the year is more under the influence of yin wood. A yin wood person does not have self confidence, so it follows the trends of the times. It does not spend money easily, it likes to save money.

The second half of the year is under the influence of yin fire. A yin fire person is also careful with money and seeks feelings of safety through care of specialists, it likes detailed explanations, it does not want to make money fast. So, the whole year will make the people not spending, trying to hold back.

Let us not forget that during the decade 2024-2033, wood dragon and wood snake are considered "no wealth" influences, affecting the financial situation of the people during the years 2024 and 2025.

However, 2025 will be the first year after 2017 that we finally see the glimpse of fire. Despite the hardships we will endure in 2025, we will see a bit of light at the end of the tunnel, even if it is not consistent yet. Snake is the first animal that contains fire.

However, it is known in Bazi astrology that snake is not reliable fire. It is the flickering fire of a candle that can be sniffed out easily depending on the winds nearby.

Some important months affecting the financial situation of the people are May, August and September 2025. August and September are not good months at all, as they remove the effect of fiery good mood totally. If there is a **financial collapse** to happen in this decade, it will be in the metal months of August, September, October 2025. Many financial specialists warn about stock market collapse, and according to my expectation, the **bursting of the financial bumble** of printed money may happen in 2025.

Regarding banking, we will see changes happening in 2025. Snake is about transformations. Banking is metal element, snake is the birth place of metal, so in 2025 we will see the **birth of banking reforms.**
I cannot imagine in what way, but it will be different from what we know.

During 2025 we might see problems with the **banks**, maybe they **reduce or cancel services.** Banks are metal, metal is weak in a wood/fire environment.

We are into Period 9 that belongs to fire element, fire melts the metal (banking) into a different shape. Metal is melted by fire flames, it becomes a new fluid element that looks like water, it gets the shape of the mold. In the next few years, starting 2025, we will see **a new banking system.** Maybe the money (metal coins) will be limited, or everything will become more electronic, even a **new type of currency** might emerge.

Religion & church

Religion is about what we have into our hearts. Yin fire is related to the heart. From 2025 and until 2027 we will be looking more into **religion/ church** matters. **Fanatism** and demonstrations about religion matters will be present, this is because snake is explosive energy.

60 years ago, catholic and orthodox **church got closer.** There were also modernization practices in the Vatican.
In 2025, for the very first time, the Catholic, Orthodox and Jewish Easter, they are all at the same day, so it could be that we see similar events.

Travel & entertainment

The snake is considered to be a "Travel Horse", it is one of the Symbolic Stars of Chinese Astrology. Many people will **travel,** move home or even country and in general welcome change.

On the other hand, the snake will bring **accidents** related to **aviation.** As the snake is a long animal, this means that we will see problems related to **railways** or **train accidents.** As snake loves to by a spy, legal cases or issues about previous train accidents will be in focus.

Arts & entertainment

Yin wood is very capable with its fingers, it is elegant and takes care of its looks (Coco Chanel was a yin wood lady). Yin wood is also the **textile** and **fashion** business, so in 2025 we will see more elegant kind of fashion. Fashion will draw the attention of the media as well in 2025, do not forget that in 1965 Mary Quant make the mini skirt popular.

Yin wood is a small plant, so **green** colors will be in focus. Other color in focus during 2025 will be all the fire colors (snake is fire element) and a touch of **metallic** and **white** and **light gray** (snake is the birth of metal).

Yin wood likes to be beautiful and takes care of its looks, so people will continue to **spend money to be good looking,** which is good news for the beauty industry. Yin wood is **vain** too.

Yin wood is charming, think how easy a beautiful flower can attract bees and insects.

Yin wood has **good manners,** so in 2025 good manners will be appreciated and in focus again.

Yin wood is creative, this is an important trait for nice art, so 2025 will be a year with nice art too. There are many yin wood people that are very skillful with their hands, they are great at tailoring and handicraft, or playing musical organs.

The fire element of the snake is related to **restaurants, movies** and **entertainment.** This will bring prosperity to the shining world of entertainment business.

Fire is also about excitement and passion, these qualities will mark 2025.

In 1965 the world was swept by Rolling Stones song " I can't get no satisfaction", by Bob Dylan's song "Like a Rolling Stone", by Tom Jones' song It's not unusual". The Beetles performed in New York the first stadium concert in music history.

Important films of 1965 were "Dr Zhivago" with Omar Sharif and "Repulsion" of Roman Polanski.

Predictions 2025
The 12 Chinese animals

If you are born in one of the following years, the new year 2025 might bring to you the following:

Tiger
If you are born in the year of the tiger, this snake year may affect you in a negative way in money matters and physical well-being. You can easily fall sick. You feel lonely. Do not start a new business. You will have a chance to prove yourself.

Rabbit
As a rabbit, you have a chance to travel this year. Many short but busy trips. You might move house, change job , travel abroad for work or find a job abroad. Embrace change. Your career may prosper. You may spend more. Accident prone. You will go to a burial.

Dragon
Everything that you want will be fulfilled. Your general fortune is good and most of the things come your way. If you are born in the year of the dragon, snake is your first shar affecting travel and money matters, so you might spend more while on the roads. Avoid visiting graves.

Snake
Do not be fooled that this is your year because it is the year of the snake. You are offending the Grand Duke Jupiter, so carry

with you during the whole year a monkey pendant. Be very careful with your friends and people you know. They might cheat you. An uncertain year.

Horse

2025 is a year that you can enjoy romance and success with the opposite sex. However take care of your health, it's a year of illness. This is not your year, be patient. Be careful of your friends. Do not lent money. Do not make important decisions. You. will travel.

Goat

You have a chance to travel this year. It is also good to move house, change job and do things that you have never done before. Embrace change. You are in power. Things will work your way. You will be offered a job of authority. Mourning year, a relative will die.

Monkey

If you are born in the year of the monkey, snake is your first shar affecting travel and money matters, so be careful with your money while on the roads. You have helpful friends. A relative may die. Be careful not to lose money. An unsettled year. Good luck with literary fame. Unexpected accidents.

Rooster

If you are born in the year of the rooster, you may be promoted to a better position. You will spend a lot of money in 2025 or you will lose money. You might even earn less money. You will be involved in accidents so be careful how you drive or when you travel.

Dog

You will be offered a better position at work. Avoid corrupt dealings. You will win a lawsuit. The dog will meet the symbolic star called Hong Luan Sha and it will bring to the dog some much needed romance or even marriage. A happy year. You will be trusted. Your problems are sorted out.

Pig

You have a chance to travel this year. It is also good to move house, change job and do things that you have never done before. Embrace change. You fortune is good, you can make sudden money from from speculation or partnership. Be aware of sudden changes of fortune, you might lose huge money. You will be mourning about a beloved one.

Rat

If you are born in the year of the rat, snake is your first shar affecting travel and money matters, so be careful. Sudden money problems. You are vulnerable to sickness or accident but you have a lucky star that will help you recover. It is a so-so year for you.

Ox

Money can come more easily this year. It is a very rewarding year money wise. There will be quarrels, even a lawsuit. Your judgement ability is impaired, you easily make wrong decisions or fall into bad influence of other people.

Note

Predictions based on the year of birth are not very reliable. The Chinese animal that is present at year of birth is only one eighth of the natal chart of a person, without taking any account the luck pillars (transits).

It is advised to consult a Bazi professional in order to take the best life decisions.

Predictions 2025 for the 10 day masters

Day Master or personal element is the heavenly stem of the day you were born. You may find your personal element in the Chinese Calendar or in any online 4 Pillars of Destiny (BaZi) calculator.

The day master can show quite some information about what a year holds for you.

Actually day master predictions are much more accurate than Chinese animal predictions, as the day master calculation is based on the specific day, month and year of birth of a person.

Chinese animal predictions are based on the year of birth. You can easily understand that not everyone born in the same year will have the same things happening.

BaZi means "8 characters". The day master and the Chinese year animal are only 2 out of the 8 characters. In addition, in BaZi we also take into consideration the "luck pillars" which are equivalent to big 10-year transits, plus the year and month influences.

Making exact predictions of a person's life needs the examination of the whole chart plus to consider the actual and present areas of interest of the person.
Get yourself a proper 4 pillars of destiny (BaZi) consultation for details and more accurate predictions.

Yang wood 甲

If you are born in the day of yang wood, it is a good year for networking with other people, in social media or other ways. Make partnerships. It's a year that is creative to you, giving you a feeling of freedom. You can do sports or start new activities and hobbies. You will spend more money somehow. You might have job difficulties, you might even change job.

If you are a woman, you might face competition in your relationship and you might have some relationship trouble caused by others.

If you are a man, you might meet a lady while travelling, but you might decide to keep it hidden. You will introduce the lady as your friend to your environment.

If you are born in the day of yang wood, this year you have the literature nobleman star, if you are a book author or if you write a study/research, you may get effective help. The heavenly kitchen star will help you enjoy a great lifestyle full of pleasures.

Yin wood 乙

You might have issues with your sisters, brothers, or colleagues, mainly of the main sex.

You may meet new friends during travelling. Other people might join you in hobby activities and sports. You might go on trips with colleagues or friends or siblings. You can enjoy some romance this year.

If you are a lady, in 2025 you might meet a new man, it can happen when you travel or when you are on the roads. A birth of a new relationship. If you are already with someone, the old relationship will have problems or it may even finish so that something new may come.

If you are a man, you may have a hidden affair during your travels or holidays, but most probably the relationship will stay hidden. Yin wood people might change jobs and find something new.

Yang fire 丙

It's a good year to get busy with decoration, renovation, buying a new home, clothes or car. You will see your mother or parents or older people, they will play a role into your life this year. Maybe these people will get exhausted.

Be careful not to lose money, yin fire is robbing money to you. Increase your security and home. Bills will be coming to you because of your big spending for resources.

It's a great year to take a seminar and expand your wisdom. You might make money through networking, although the money is weak at the beginning.

Yang fire day master has the Heaven Luck Nobleman star this year, this helps especially with career matters, so it is good to go ahead in career matters.

Also the Correct Measure Nobleman star will help you to be lucky if you have a correct private life without extremes.

Yin fire 丁

If you are born in the day of yin fire, you might find yourself learning new things or finishing your studies. It is your last chance to study well, as it is the last year in the next few years that wood is present. It is good to do unusual studies such as astrology, music, herbal medicine etc.

You may spend money for your home decoration, or you might decide to buy a new house, renew your clothes garderobe etc. It's a money spending year.

Your mother, your siblings and your colleagues will be in your focus during 2025. Good for networking and making new friends. You may get money only through partnerships but the results will take time to grow.

Yang earth 戊

As a yang earth day master, you will be busy with your job in 2025, you might even find a new one. If fire element is favorable to you, you will very successful in career matters. If fire element is unfavorable to you, you will get frustrated with your job and also be careful with your health.

It's a good year to do seminars, take care of your nutrition or do renovations at home or renew your garderobe.

If you are a lady, you might meet a new man or your relationship will draw your attention, you might travel with him or have holidays travelling. If you like fire, you will have a good time with your other half, but if you don't like fire you will want to escape the relationship.

Yin earth 己

Yin earth days masters, you will see similar things happening to you like the yang earth day masters. Read my comments above to get ideas.

In addition to that written above, in 2025 you will find yourself stretching your reflexes this year and be very defensive because you might feel stressed/attacked or under pressure, you might feel that your boss is a bit harsh, see it as an opportunity to train yourself and get better. However if fire element is good for you, fire will help you relax in the long term.

Yang metal 庚

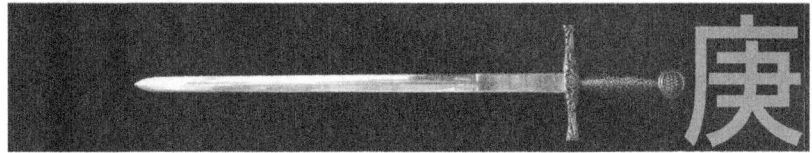

If you are born in the day of yang metal, in 2025 you will see some money coming your way, but you will also spend a lot of it. You will find yourself busy with your job full time. If you like fire, you will like the job, but if you do not like fire you might lose your patience and feel too much pressure with it.

Yang metal people will also focus in their father this year.

If you are a yang metal man, things will happen in your relationship. You might meet a new person. If you already have a problematic relationship, there is the possibility to break it up especially in April, May or even September.

Yin metal 辛

As a yin metal person, you may see unexpected money, especially if you like fire element. As you love luxury, you might spend a lot of money too. Your father is brought into your attention. It is also a year that you will be working for someone or a company, so if you are looking for a job this year you can find something more stable that will last.

Yang metal lady, you will have a relationship in 2025, you like it or not. Be aware however that this man might be hiding another lady, keeping her secret from you. You have the heaven power nobleman star this year, you have protection in case you are involved in legal conflicts. You also have the private luck nobleman, so you can enjoy personal or family happiness.

Yang water 壬

If you are a yang water day master, this year you will be creative, you can even make yourself more known, you know how to present yourself and make a good impression. You might do some more fitness than usual. It's a year when you get things done. Money is your main issue in 2025, if you like fire element you will increase your income. But if you don't like fire element, you will struggle with money.

A yang water man will have a relationship. A yang water woman might meet someone during trips and if you are planning to have a child give a try for giving birth in 2025.

If you are born in the day or year of yang water, this is your nobleman year. You have a helping hand from other people, especially those born in the day or year of the rabbit or snake. Also a "guardian angel" or proper circumstances help you get out of trouble. You may ask favors this year that will be answered positively. Luck in the unkuck.

Yin water 癸

Yin water day masters, 2025 is your creativity and money year. If you like fire, you will be able to make great profit, also try your luck with unexpected ways to increase your income, think big. But if you don't like fire, you might lose money or might find it hard to save.

For a man it is relationship year, if you are single you may start something new.

For a woman, she might meet someone new as well, try your luck while on your way. For ladies this year can bring you a child.

Yin water people will also enjoy the benefits of the "Nobleman" star in 2025. People or circumstances will help you get out of trouble. If you ask for help or favors, other will help you. Especially positive people to you are those born in the day or year of the rabbit or the snake.

Even if you face obstacles, for yin water people there is luck in the unluck.

Date Selection 2025

Date Selection

How to use Date Selection
9 steps to success

Read all the steps below, from 1 to 9. The main idea about choosing a good date is first to take away all the bad dates, see what days are left, then choose the day with the best energy.

When I do Date Selection, in order to save time, I go to the Tong Shu section with the tables, I take a pencil and I first mark out with an X all the bad dates (I put an X inside the bad boxes of specific days).

Then, from what is left, I write these better days down on a piece of paper and analyze them in detail. I choose for example the day that is matching my activity, I check if it is good for me (matching my chinese animal, a day with my good element, a day with nobleman etc).
I also pay attention to the hour, as sometimes the day is good but the hour is against the day or myself.

Step 1 - clash
First you find the days that are clashing with you. Clash is the day that fights against you, you do not want that. Clash brings obstacles and conflict.
Mark with your pencil an X on the "clash" box if you see there written your chinese animal of year of birth.

Clash means also travel, clash makes you move out of your place, you will observe that there is anyway a tendency to travel when the day is clashing with the chinese animal of your year of birth, again it is wise to follow the rest of date selection steps.

For medical Date Selection I suggest you look for a 4 pillars or astrology specialist, as each body part belongs to an element and one must check the whole 4 pillars of a person. Just for your information, choosing a day that clashes with your day branch (also known as house of spouse), might be OK if you are having an operation, as a clash against your body under a medical specialist is anyway a kind of physical attack by itself.

Step 2 - 12 Rulers - The quality of the day

Each day belongs to a Ruler. The ruler talk about the general energy of that day. There are in total 12 rulers.

The 12 rulers are actually related to the 12 phases you have to go through when you start a project. In the old times, it was like the Chinese farmer that goes to a new place with his family and caravan, in order to establish himself and live there for ever.

First you "establish" youself by saying you want to start your project, then you do "removal" by removing the obstacles,enemies already there, then you "fulfil" because your hands are now full and things are at their maximum, then you "balance" things out because you have to negotiate with others on equal footing, then "stability" because only now you start exact planning of your long term project, then "control" which is the day that clashes the month which brings unexpected instability and bad luck to your project and so on.

Select the day with the appropriate Ruler, first avoid the negative Rulers for your activity. Mark with an X the negative Rulers. Find a good Ruler using common sense.

In short, I give you some quick indications about best Rulers for common activities:

Marriage: Accomplishment, Stability and Opening.
Divorce request, or remove a partner: Removal.
Starting diet: Removal and Accomplishment.
New business: Opening, Accomplishment, Fulfilment and Stability.
Negotiations: Accomplishment, Stability, Fulfilment and Harvest.
Sign contracts: Balance, Accomplishment, Stability.
Travel: Accomplishment, Fulfilment, Balance.
Medical operation: Removal, Stability or Balance
   (idepending on what the operation is doing to your body).

The 12 Rulers follow this sequence:

1.	**Establish**	建
2.	**Removal**	除
3.	**Fulfil**	滿
4.	**Balance**	平
5.	**Stability**	定
6.	**Control**	執
7.	**Clash**	破
8.	**Danger**	危
9.	**Accomplish**	成
10.	**Harvest**	收
11.	**Opening**	開
12.	**Closing**	閉

1. Establish 建
It is the day that has the same earthly branch like the month. It's the day you show your intention.

Suitable for engagement, marriage proposal, visiting friends, establish communication, start new job, start new seminar, discuss business, start medical exams, seek medical treatment, make travel plans, travel, start construction. Avoid ground breaking, funeral, burial.

2. Removal 除

Remove what you don't want in your life. Suitable to end a bad relationship, start diet (remove kilos), remove things from your body medically, cleanse your space, Removal also means getting rid of bad luck and bad karma, thus it is good for pest control and catching a thief. Avoid adopting a child, buying a pet, marriage.

3. Fulfil 滿

Everything is full. Suitable to sign contract, collect dept (the full amount), official opening, party (everyone comes), install new equipment (fully), launch new campaign. Avoid marriage, start lawsuit & court, sign contract full of list of obligations, start a new job (full of responsibilities), burial.

4. Balance 平

It's a day good for negotiation if you are the weaker side or if you wish a win win result. Outcome is balanced but not advantageous. If you are the stronger party, in a balance day this will favor the weaker. Suitable to marriage, travel, construction, business negotiations. Avoid to start a legal action (result will favour both sides), distribution of wealth, make a will, divide assets, burial.

5. Stability 定

This day has lasting effects. Suitable for marriage (for ever), business agreement, finalize things for ever. Official opening, start construction, hire, buy a pet, make party, seek medical treatment (permanent cure). Avoid to move home (or you will be moving for ever), travel, funeral, burial, start a job (or you stay at this position there for ever). Avoid a project that you want to do fast.

6. Control 執

It's the day you start your intented activity, new beginnings. It's a day with average energy, as it's the day before destruction. Also known as Initiate day. Suitable to start new project, open business, renovate house, start ground breaking. Avoid moving into new home, travel (unless your intention is the trip and not the destination).

7. Clash 破

This day is in clash with the month. Clash means something external out of control comes and destroys. The worse day of all. Also known as destruction day. Suitable to demolish a building, diet (you destroy and break free from bad habits for ever). Avoid marriage, open business, start a trip, sign contract, engagement as all these activities will be totally destroyed, there is no turning back. Do not resign that day, as you might need to work with these people again in the future, if you have chosen a clash day, the business relationship is destroyed and you wont be able to do it. It's a nasty unstable day.

8. Danger 危

I's a dangerous day, everything is uncertain. Suitable for religious worship, fix bed, dismandle objects, ground breaking. Avoid sports, risky activities, travel, move house, marriage, burial.

9. Accomplish 成

It is the best day of all Rulers, you have a positive outcome. It is also known as success day. Suitable to get married, seek medical treatment, submit business proposal, construct, move home, burial. Suitable for all good activities. Avoid bad activities, eg lawsuits or you will have more lawsuits with success.

10. Harvest 收
Also known as receive day. It's a day of harvest and getting rewards. Use it if you want to ask something in return. Suitable to start a new job, start a new school, ask for pay raise, close a deal, marriage proposal. Avoid to seek medical treatment (or you get even more treatments), visit sick people (or you also get sick), construction, attending funeral, burial.

11. Opening 開
A very auspicious day for activities that relate to opening or welcoming. Suitable to open business, house warming, new job, start work after long break, sign contracts, new school, marriage. Avoid burial and ground breaking.

12. Closing 閉
It's a day will low energy. Never select a close day. It closes things. Avoid acupuncture. Suitable for job resignation, burial.

Step 3 - Influence
Bad energy on that day because of the month and the year.
The Tong Shu has a section with the name "Influence". In that box I have calculated all the bad influences of the day with the month and the year. I put numbered bombs for easy reference. Some days have bombs, and they have bad energies, some days do not have any bombs.
I have calculated for your behalf 6 types of bad energies, so you will see 6 types of bombs.

The meaning of the "bombs":

❶ Year clash is the day that clashes with the year. Avoid this day as this means that the activity is under clash with the year and it will have obstacles as long as the activity lasts. Your activity may not come to fruition or even have reverse effect. Choose it only if you don't mind to be hurt or if you have nothing to lose.

❷ Month clash is the day that clashes with the month. As the day pillar is close to the month pillar, this clash is very strong and serious. Avoid selecting a day with month clash as its easy that this activity will "break" easily leading to complicated and difficult situations.

❸ 3 Shars with the year is the day that is in 3 Shar relationship with the year. 3 Shars bring accidents, misfortune and illness. This day is not as negative as the "bombs" 1 and 2.

❹ 3 Shars with the month is the day that is in 3 Shar relationship with the month. 3 Shars bring accidents, misfortune and illness. Also this "bomb" is not as bad as bombs 1 and 2.

❺ 4 Separation days are the days before Spring Equinox 春分, Autumn Equinox 秋分, Summer Solstice 夏至 και Winter Solstice 冬至. These are days with weak energy. Not good for marriage, move house, travel, construction.

❻ 4 Termination days are the day before "Arrival of Spring" 立春, "Arrival of Summer" 立夏, "Arrival of Autumn" 立秋 and "Arrival of Winter" 立冬. These are days with weak energy. Not good of marriage, move house, travel, construction.

❼ No wealth days. Avoid signing contracts, business trading & decisions, investments, financial opening, business trips.

Step 4 - Good activities - Bad activities

In the Tong Shu you will see a box that says good, and a box that says bad. If the Tong Shu says that your desired activity is bad that day please do not choose it. If the Tong Shu says that your desired activity is good, then this is another plus factor to choose that day, if also the other steps to date selection agree choosing that day. If you don't see your activity, then it is not a bad day at least, so its OK.

Step 5 - Flying star of day
Feng Shui for the day

In the Tong Shu you will see there is a box that says "Flying Star", and there is also a number there (from 1 to 9). That number is the central flying star of the day, consultant know how to "fly" it and find what are the influences in the other directions. You apply this step only if you want to find a day with good Feng Shui at the door of the buidling: move house, open ceremony, demolition, construction, renovation etc.

If your activity involves a building, you do not want to have the Flying Star 5 at the door of your apartment or office or shop. Find in the Tong Shu tables the box with the name "Flying Star". What is the Flying Star of that day? Now find where is Star 5 that day.

The Table below shows you the location of the daily Flying Star 5:

Flying star of the day	Star 5
1	South
2	Northeast
3	West
4	Northwest
5	Center
6	Southeast
7	East
8	Southwest
9	North

Step 6 - The nobleman star
How to have a helping hand
Nobleman is an energy that acts like a helping hand in your life. Someone comes to help you when you need something or when you are in trouble. You may find your own nobleman from the table below:

Heavenly stems of year or day of birth	Nobleman star
甲　　戊　　庚 yang wood　yang earth　yang metal	丑　　未 Ox　　Goat
乙　　己 yin wood　yin earth	子　　申 Rat　　Monkey
丙　　丁 yang fire　yin fire	亥　　酉 Pig　　Rooster
壬　　癸 Yang water　yin water	卯　　巳 Rabbit　　Snake
辛 yin metal	午　　寅 Horse　　Tiger

If you are new to chinese astrology and you do not understand the table above, here is another way to apply it:
- If your birth year has last digit 4, 8 or 0, your nobleman is the ox and the goat.
- If your birth year has last digit 5 or 9, your nobleman is the rat and the monkey.
- If your birth year has last digit 2 or 3, your nobleman is the rabbit and the snake.
- If your birth year has last digit 1, your nobleman is the horse and the tiger.
- If your birth year has last digit 6 or 7, your noblmean is the pig and the rooster.

For important activities, choose a month, day or hour with your nobleman star.

Note: If you were born between 1 January and 3rd February, use the previous digit to find your nobleman. This is because in 4 pillars astrology we use usually the 4th of February as beginning of the year. 1st of January belongs to the previous year.

Step 7 - Favourable elements & the 10 Gods
Choosing a day with your favourable elements is a very good thing, it means it will be a smooth day. If a day has the elements that are good for you, things will be "lucky", things will go easy and well. You can find out your favorable and unfavorable elements only if you do a consultation with a 4 pillars expert. You may also choose a day related to your own 10 Gods. For example, if your activity has to do with money, you may choose a money day. If it has to do with diet, you choose resources, if you are a woman getting married, you choose the day that has the element that represents your husband etc. This is a step that can only be followed by a professional consultant.

Step 8 - 3 Shar and Death Angel
To take Date Selection into a further level, you may also consider to avoid the day that is in 3 Shar relationship with you, and you may also avoid the day that is your Death Angel.
- The first Shar creates robbery, loss of money and is often related to travel (its always a travel horse direction).
- The second Shar creates injury, illness, sex problems or excessive sex (its always a peach blossom direction).

- The third Shar creates delays, obstacles, being stuck, loneliness (it is always an earth grave direction). It is less serious than the other shars. Death Angel brings accidents or legal trouble.

3 Shar

- If you are born in the year of the monkey, rat, dragon:
  Avoid the day of the snake (1st Shar), horse (2nd Shar) and goat (3rd Shar).
- If you are born in the year of the tiger, horse, dog:
  Avoid the day of the pig (1st Shar), rat (2n Shar) and ox (3rd Shar).
- If you are born in the year of the snake, rooster, ox:
  Avoid the day of the tiger (1st Shar), rabbit (2nd Shar), and dragon (3rd Shar).
- If you are born in the year of the pig, rabbit, goat:
  Avoid the day of the monkey (1st Shar), rooster (2nd Shar) and dog (3rd Shar).

Death angel

- If you are born in the year of the monkey, rat, dragon:
  Avoid the day of the pig, the pig is your personal Death Angel.
- If you are born in the year of the tiger, horse, dog:
  Avoid the day of the snake, the snake is your personal Death Angel.
- If you are born in the year of the pig, rabbit, goat:
  Avoid the day of tiger, the tiger is your personal Death Angel.
- If you are born in the year of the snake, rooster, ox:
  Avoid the day of the monkey, the monkey is your personal Death Angel.
- If you are born in the year of the pig, rabbit, goat: Avoid the day of the monkey (1st Shar), rooster (2nd shar) and dog (3rd shar).

Step 9 - how to select the perfect hour

First choose the right day, then choose the right hour. If you cannot choose the right day, then at least choose a good hour.

The basic rules to select a good hour:

✓Avoid the hour that clashes with the day of your choice
Consult the table below.

Chinese animal of the day	Hours that clash with day	
寅 Tiger	申 Monkey	15.00-17.00
卯 Rabbit	酉 Rooster	17.00-19.00
辰 Dragon	戌 Dog	19.00-21.00
巳 Snake	亥 Pig	21.00-23.00
午 Horse	子 Rat	23.00-01.00
未 Goat	丑 Ox	01.00-03.00
申 Monkey	寅 Tiger	03.00-05.00
酉 Rooster	卯 Rabbit	05.00-07.00
戌 Dog	辰 Dragon	07.00-09.00
亥 Pig	巳 Snake	09.00-11.00
子 Rat	午 Horse	11.00-13.00
丑 Ox	未 Goat	13.00-15.00

Example: The day of the tiger, avoid the hour of the monkey.
Because that day, the day is fighting against the hour, you don't want that.

✓Avoid the hour that clashes with your Chinese animal sign
Consult the table below.

Chinese animal of your birth year	Hours that clash with your year of birth
寅 Tiger	申 Monkey 15.00-17.00
卯 Rabbit	酉 Rooster 17.00-19.00
辰 Dragon	戌 Dog 19.00-21.00
巳 Snake	亥 Pig 21.00-23.00
午 Horse	子 Rat 23.00-01.00
未 Goat	丑 Ox 01.00-03.00
申 Monkey	寅 Tiger 03.00-05.00
酉 Rooster	卯 Rabbit 05.00-07.00
戌 Dog	辰 Dragon 07.00-09.00
亥 Pig	巳 Snake 09.00-11.00
子 Rat	午 Horse 11.00-13.00
丑 Ox	未 Goat 13.00-15.00

Example: If you are born in the year of the tiger, do not choose the hour of the monkey, you are clashing against that hour.

✓ Use the Tong Shu to find good, average and bad hours.
Go to the end of the book, (pages 192-203).
I have a special section with the Tong Shu hours for every day of the year. The hours mentioned there are real solar hours, this means that before you use this table you need to do the 2 steps corrections I mention just below.

✓ Choose a nobleman hour. Find your nobleman at page 89.
The table below shows the chinese animals and what hours they occupy.

Nobleman animals	Nobleman hours
寅 Tiger	03.00-05.00
卯 Rabbit	05.00-07.00
辰 Dragon	07.00-09.00
巳 Snake	09.00-11.00
午 Horse	11.00-13.00
未 Goat	13.00-15.00
申 Monkey	15.00-17.00
酉 Rooster	17.00-19.00
戌 Dog	19.00-21.00
亥 Pig	21.00-23.00
子 Rat	23.00-01.00
丑 Ox	01.00-03.00

Example: If your nobleman is the tiger, choose the hour 03.00-05.00. Always remember that you must correct,change the hour, depending on the city that the event will take place. This means that the real tiger hour might not be 03-05am in your city. Below you see how to do that.

✓ **Change the time into real solar time at any city.** The hour shown on your watch is not the real solar hour. You need to know the solar hour, the solar hour is the real hour of the nature.
Two steps have to be made to find the real solar time of a city.
• If summer time applies, convert it to winter time (winter time = minus 1 hour from the summer time). Summer time is artificial. Your calculation

must be based on winter time. You need to find out if that country applies Daylight Saving the day of the activity.
* Find the real time at that city and not the conventional artificial time of the time zone or country. You need to know at that city, what hour exactly is the sun exactly above the city without any shadows. At the end of the book, you will se the appendix with the solar time for major world cities. If at the table next to the city you see a plus (+), add the minutes shown. If you see a minus (-), subtract these minutes.

If you don't find your city in my list, there is an excellent and accurate website that calculates Solar Noon for any minor city of the planet and also includes if there was summer time or not.

> **www.timeanddate.com, sun and moon, sun calculator, just type the country and city of your request**

Example of correcting the hour

You want to get married at 20.00. The marriage will take place in Athens in June, in June in Greece there is summer time.

- **Step 1:** make summer time to winter time: 20.00 summer time is actually 19.00 winter time.
- **Step 2:** Find the appendix table with the main world cities, it says Athens is -25 minutes. Subtract 25 minutes from the previous result: 19.00-25 minutes= 18.35 pm.
* Find from table above what Chinese animal governs that hour: 18.35pm is the hour of the rooster.
* Find the Tong Shu table section, is that hour that specific day, a good, bad or average hour?

TONG SHU 2025

About the Tong Shu

Tong Shu or the Book of Myriad Things is the book with the longest continuous printed history of any other book in the world.

In 2256 BC Emperor Yao commanded his officials to write a book that correlated lunar and solar dates and gives advice the ordinary people. According to other Taoist traditions, the calendar was invented even earlier by Fu Hsi, a semi human semi divine figure. This book was meant to control the heavens and the seasons. Initially it had a totally agricultural basis. Through the centuries, it has been reformed and expanded many times.

Today, its purpose is to choose the best day and hour for all kind of activities: marriage, moving home, travel, open business, even cut hair. The traditional Tong Shu also contains a lot of other information such as stories, tables, charms, predictions, divination, Chinese face reading etc.

There are few Chinese homes that do not have a copy of the Tong Shu. However, is not understood fully by ordinary Chinese. They still go to a specialist when they must choose real important activities like marriage and opening a new business.

The Tong Shu section of book you have in your hands right now, it incorporates information of the classical Tong Shu, together with Date Selection methods. This way you can do DIY use of the Tong Shu.

I also calculated for your behalf the section "Influence", that you don't normally find it in any other Tong Shu. That section tells you in form of little "bombs" energies that are universal unfavorable, these are days that interact badly with the year, season or month. This way you don't have to calculate it yourself every time you want to find a good date.

You will notice that once you follow all the methods I mention in this book, you will not find many good dates for the activity you desire. This is normal, there are not many good days, especially when you have time limitation or there are many people involved in the activity eg a marriage on a Sunday.

However, choosing a good day and good hour can ensure a smooth operation of the activity and will enhance its chances of success in the future.

I know many people that are not patient to go through all the steps of date selection and just select a good hour. This is also better than nothing.

January

1 Wednesday 庚午 Metal Horse	Clash	Influence	12 Rulers	Flying star
	Rat	❷ ❸ ❹	Clash	7
	Good		**Bad**	
	Demolish, Break Floor		Think Thrice	

2 Thursday 辛未 Metal Goat	Clash	Influence	12 Rulers	Flying star
	Ox	❸ ❹	Danger	8
	Good		**Bad**	
	Logging, Hunting		Major Moves	

3 Friday 壬申 Water Monkey	Clash	Influence	12 Rulers	Flying star
	Tiger		Accomplish	9
	Good		**Bad**	
	Engagement, Pray, Pay Tribute, Marriage, Opening, Pray for Progeny, Visiting relatives, Sign contract, Gathering, Cut hair, New school, Clean house, Travel, Acupuncture, New Job, Burial, Move House		Fix Sewage, Fix Bed, Fix Floor, Repair House	

4 Saturday 癸酉 Water Rooster	Clash	Influence	12 Rulers	Flying star
	Rabbit		Harvest	1
	Good		**Bad**	
	Ritual bath, Cut hair, Cut Nail, Clean Floor, Pest Control, Hunting		Buy House, Opening, Payment, Sign contract	

January

5 Sunday 甲戌 Wood Dog	Clash Dragon	Influence 💣 *	12 Rulers Harvest	Flying star 2
	Good Pray, Pest Control, Hunting		Bad Marriage, Move House, Buy House, Burial	

6 Monday 乙亥 Wood Pig	Clash Snake	Influence	12 Rulers Opening	Flying star 3
	Good Visiting relatives, Pray, Gathering, Pay Tribute, New school, Clean house, Pray for Progeny, Sewing, Repair House, Opening, New Construction, Buy House, Cast Beam, Herding, Dig Well, Take Animal, Shipments			Bad Travel, Marriage, Return Home Land, Move House

7 Tuesday 丙子 Fire Rat	Clash Horse	Influence	12 Rulers Closing	Flying star 4
	Good Pray, Ritual bath, Acupuncture, Brew Wine, Burial		Bad Opening, Marriage, New Construction, Sign contract	

8 Wednesday 丁丑 Fire Ox	Clash Goat	Influence	12 Rulers Establish	Flying star 5
	Good Pray, Fix Altar		Bad Think Thrice, Except above	

* 5 JAN - Bomb 1: Valid 24 hours

January

9 **Thursday** 戊寅 **Earth Tiger**	Clash Monkey	Influence ❹	12 Rulers Removal	Flying star 6
	Good Ritual bath, Clean Floor			Bad Pray, Travel, Burial, Break Ground

10 **Friday** 己卯 **Earth Rabbit**	Clash Rooster	Influence ❹	12 Rulers Fulfill	Flying star 7
	Good Pray			Bad Be Conservative

11 **Saturday** 庚辰 **Metal Dragon**	Clash Dog	Influence ❹	12 Rulers Balance	Flying star 8
	Good Pray, Repair Road			Bad Marriage, Travel, Opening, Burial

12 **Sunday** 辛巳 **Metal Snake**	Clash Pig	Influence ❸	12 Rulers Stability	Flying star 9
	Good Visiting relatives, Pray, Gathering, Pay Tribute, New Job, Wedding gift, Pray for Progeny, Mitzvah, Move House, Sewing, Repair House, Sign contract, New Construction, Herding, Acupuncture, Take Animal, Fix warehouse			Bad Travel, Marriage, Boating, Burial

January

13 Monday 壬午 Water Horse	Clash Rat	Influence ❸		12 Rulers Control	Flying star 1
	Good Ritual bath, Cut hair, Cut Nail, Logging, Pest Control, Hunting			Bad Pay Tribute, Marriage, Burial, Opening	

14 Tuesday 癸未 Water Goat	Clash Ox	Influence ❷ ❸		12 Rulers Clash	Flying star 2
	Good Pray, Demolish, Break Floor			Bad Think Thrice	

15 Wednesday 甲申 Wood Monkey	Clash Tiger	Influence		12 Rulers Danger	Flying star 3
	Good Pray, Repair House, New Construction, Travel, Fix warehouse, Move House, Brew Wine, Ritual bath, Cut hair, Opening, Collect Money, Clean Floor, Cut Nail, Sewing, Burial			Bad Marriage, Delivery, Pay Tribute, Fix Bed	

16 Thursday 乙酉 Wood Rooster	Clash Rabbit	Influence		12 Rulers Accomplish	Flying star 4
	Good Pray, Move House, Cut hair, Pay Tribute, Pray for Progeny, Cut Nail, Travel, Opening, Wedding gift, Sign contract, Propose marriage, Trading, Marriage, Sewing, Burial			Bad Hunting, Fishing, Visiting relatives, Planting, Gathering	

January

17 **Friday** 丙戌 **Fire Dog**	**Clash** Dragon	**Influence** ❶	**12 Rulers** Harvest	**Flying star** 5
	Good Pray, Pest Control, Hunting		**Bad** Build Oven, Sign contract	

18 **Saturday** 丁亥 **Fire Pig**	**Clash** Snake	**Influence**	**12 Rulers** Opening	**Flying star** 6
	Good Pray, New school, Ritual bath		**Bad** Cut hair, Travel, Cut hair, Marriage	

19 **Sunday** 戊子 **Earth Rat**	**Clash** Horse	**Influence**	**12 Rulers** Closing	**Flying star** 7
	Good Pray, Ritual bath		**Bad** Move House, Travel, Visiting relatives, Fix Bed, Gathering	

20 **Monday** 己丑 **Earth Ox**	**Clash** Goat	**Influence**	**12 Rulers** Establish	**Flying star** 8
	Good Sewing		**Bad** Demolish, Repair Road, Break Floor	

January

21 Tuesday 庚寅 Metal Tiger	Clash: Monkey	Influence: ❹	12 Rulers: Removal	Flying star: 9
	Good: Engagement, Visiting relatives, Gathering, Marriage, New Job, New Construction, Move House, Clean house, Repair House, Cut hair, Sign contract, Take Animal, Cut Nail, Planting, Break Ground, Clean Floor, Burial			**Bad**: Hunting, Pray, Fishing, Travel

22 Wednesday 辛卯 Metal Rabbit	Clash: Rooster	Influence: ❹	12 Rulers: Fulfill	Flying star: 1
	Good: Pray			**Bad**: Engagement, Pay Tribute, Wedding gift, Pray for Progeny

23 Thursday 壬辰 Water Dragon	Clash: Dog	Influence: ❹	12 Rulers: Balance	Flying star: 2
	Good: Be Careful			**Bad**: Major Changes, Be Conservative

24 Friday 癸巳 Water Snake	Clash: Pig	Influence: ❸	12 Rulers: Stability	Flying star: 3
	Good: Visiting relatives, Repair House, Gathering, Mitzvah, New Construction, Engagement, Cast Beam, Brew Wine, Wedding gift, Sign contract, Propose marriage, Acupuncture, Take Animal, Adoption			**Bad**: Buy House, Travel, Casting Marriage

January

25 Saturday 甲午 Wood Horse	Clash Rat	Influence ❸	12 Rulers Control	Flying star 4
	Good Pray, Ritual bath, Logging, Cut hair, Cut Nail, Pest Control, Hunting		Bad Break Ground, Burial	

26 Sunday 乙未 Wood Goat	Clash Ox	Influence ❷ ❸	12 Rulers Clash	Flying star 5
	Good Pray, Clean house, Demolish, Break Floor		Bad Marriage, Repair House, Buy House, Opening	

27 Monday 丙申 Fire Monkey	Clash Tiger	Influence	12 Rulers Danger	Flying star 6
	Good Pray, Opening, Delivery, Ritual bath, Cut hair, Payment, Hunting, Cut Nail, Planting, Acupuncture, Brew Wine, Take Animal, Clean Floor, Break Ground, Logging, Burial		Bad Pay Tribute, Fix Bed, Engagement, Pray for Progeny	

28 Tuesday 丁酉 Fire Rooster	Clash Rabbit	Influence	12 Rulers Accomplish	Flying star 7
	Good Engagement, Receive award, Marriage, New school, Repair House, Travel, Opening, Move House, Clean house, Sign contract, Take Animal, Cut Nail, Break Ground, Build Dam		Bad Visiting relatives, Gathering, Cut hair	

January

29 Wednesday 戊戌 Earth Dog	Clash: Dragon	Influence: ☉	12 Rulers: Harvest	Flying star: 8
	Good: Pray, Pest Control, Hunting			Bad: Fix Sewage, Opening, Dig Well, Sign contract

30 Thursday 己亥 Earth Pig	Clash: Snake	Influence:	12 Rulers: Opening	Flying star: 9
	Good: Pray, New school, Logging			Bad: Pay Tribute, Marriage, Burial, Pray for Progeny

31 Friday 庚子 Metal Rat	Clash: Horse	Influence:	12 Rulers: Closing	Flying star: 1
	Good: Pray, Ritual bath, Sewing, Brew Wine, Burial			Bad: Buy House, Move House, Return Home Land, Break Ground

February

1 Saturday 辛丑 Metal Ox	Clash: Goat	Influence:	12 Rulers: Establish	Flying star: 2
	Good: Engagement, Pray, Pay Tribute, Wedding gift, Propose marriage, Pray for Progeny, Erect pole, Visiting relatives, Gathering, Clean house, Cast Beam, Sewing, Collect Money, Herding, Delivery			Bad: Repair House, Receive award, Mitzvah, Build Dam

February

2 **Sunday** 壬寅 **Water Tiger**	Clash Monkey	Influence ④ ⑥	12 Rulers Removal	Flying star 3
	Good Ritual bath, Clean Floor		Bad Pray, Fix warehouse, Fix Sewage, Travel	

3 **Monday** 癸卯 **Water Rabbit**	Clash Rooster	Influence ③ * ④	12 Rulers Fulfill	Flying star 4
	Good Pray		Bad Opening, Fix Bed, Burial, Marriage	

4 **Tuesday** 甲辰 **Wood Dragon**	Clash Dog	Influence ③ ⑦	12 Rulers Fulfill	Flying star 5
	Good Pray, Pay Tribute, Receive award, Policy review, Visiting relatives, Gathering, Sewing, Acupunctur		Bad Opening, Marriage, Boating, Burial	

5 **Wednesday** 乙巳 **Wood Snake**	Clash Pig	Influence ⑦	12 Rulers Balance	Flying star 6
	Good Repair Road		Bad Travel, Marriage, Opening, Sign contract	

** 3 FEB - Bomb 4: Valid **before** 22:12*

February

6 Thursday 丙午 Fire Horse	Clash Rat	Influence	12 Rulers Stability	Flying star 7
	Good Pray, Marriage, Pay Tribute, Wedding gift, Visiting relatives, Move House, Gathering, Clean house, Travel, Sewing, New Job, Repair House, Opening, Planting, Sign contract, Burial, Break Ground			Bad Visit Doctor, Hunting, Fishing

7 Friday 丁未 Fire Goat	Clash Ox	Influence	12 Rulers Control	Flying star 8
	Good Visiting relatives, Pray, Gathering, Pay Tribute, Travel, New Job, Pray for Progeny, Sewing, Move House, Planting, Repair House, New Construction, Payment, Pest Control, Herding			Bad Cut hair, Marriage, Hunting, Fishing

8 Saturday 戊申 Earth Monkey	Clash Tiger	Influence ❷	12 Rulers Clash	Flying star 9
	Good Pray, Clean house, Ritual bath, Visit Doctor, Recuperate, Clean Floor, Demolish, Break Floor			Bad Travel, Marriage, Burial, Move House

9 Sunday 己酉 Earth Rooster	Clash Rabbit	Influence	12 Rulers Danger	Flying star 1
	Good Pray, Ritual bath, Cut hair, Cut Nail, Clean Floor, Fishing, Break Ground, Burial			Bad Visiting relatives, Gathering, Travel, Marriage, Opening

February

10 Monday 庚戌 Metal Dog	Clash: Dragon	Influence:	12 Rulers: Accomplish	Flying star: 2
	Good New school			**Bad** Fix Bed, Marriage, Burial, Sign contract

11 Tuesday 辛亥 Metal Pig	Clash: Snake	Influence: ❶ ❹	12 Rulers: Harvest	Flying star: 3
	Good Pray, Move House, Visiting relatives, Pay Tribute, Gathering, New Job, Wedding gift, Sewing, Ritual bath, Repair House, Opening, Cast Beam, Sign contract, Pest Control, Payment, Planting, Take Animal			**Bad** Brew Wine, Marriage, Hunting, Fishing,

12 Wednesday 壬子 Water Rat	Clash: Horse	Influence: ❹	12 Rulers: Opening	Flying star: 4
	Good Pray, Marriage, Pay Tribute, Move House, Clean house, New school, Travel, Ritual bath, New Job, Opening, Buy House, Collect Money, Planting, Fix warehouse, Herding, Take Animal			**Bad** Logging, Fix Sewage, Hunting, Fishing

13 Thursday 癸丑 Water Ox	Clash: Goat	Influence: ❹	12 Rulers: Closing	Flying star: 5
	Good Visiting relatives, Gathering			**Bad** Think Thrice, Except above

118

February

14 Friday
甲寅
Wood Tiger

Clash	Influence	12 Rulers	Flying star
Monkey	③	Establish	6

Good: Visiting relatives, Gathering, Sewing, Sign contract, Trading, Collect Money, Take Animal

Bad: Pray, Marriage, Pay Tribute, Burial

15 Saturday
乙卯
Wood Rabbit

Clash	Influence	12 Rulers	Flying star
Rooster	③	Removal	7

Good: Engagement, Receive award, Visiting relatives, Gathering, Cut Nail, Travel, Sign contract, New Job, Trading, New Job, Clean Floor, Clean house, Break Ground, Ritual bath, Cut hair, Burial

Bad: Dig Well, Planting

16 Sunday
丙辰
Fire Dragon

Clash	Influence	12 Rulers	Flying star
Dog	③	Fulfill	8

Good: Engagement, Pray, Pay Tribute, Marriage, Repair House, Pray for Progeny, Visiting relatives, New Construction, Gathering, Opening, Travel, Sign contract, New Job, Take Animal, Move House, Acupuncture, Burial

Bad: Fix Floor, Casting Boating, Fill Hole

17 Monday
丁巳
Fire Snake

Clash	Influence	12 Rulers	Flying star
Pig		Balance	9

Good: Pray, Repair Road

Bad: Pay Tribute, Travel, Cut hair, Pray for Progeny

February

18 **Tuesday** 戊午 **Earth Horse**	Clash Rat	Influence	12 Rulers Stability	Flying star 1
	Good Engagement, Pray, Pay Tribute, Marriage, Repair House, Pray for Progeny, Visiting relatives, New Construction, Gathering, Opening, Travel, Mitzvah, Sign contract, Take Animal, New Job, Brew Wine, Move House			Bad Buy House, Clean house, Planting

19 **Wednesday** 己未 **Earth Goat**	Clash Ox	Influence	12 Rulers Control	Flying star 2
	Good Pest Control, Fishin			Bad Engagement, Opening, Sign contract, Marriage

20 **Thursday** 庚申 **Metal Monkey**	Clash Tiger	Influence ②	12 Rulers Clash	Flying star 3
	Good Demolish, Break Floor			Bad Major Moves

21 **Friday** 辛酉 **Metal Rooster**	Clash Rabbit	Influence	12 Rulers Danger	Flying star 4
	Good Logging, Hunting			Bad Boating, Demolish, Break Floor, Fishing

February

22 Saturday 壬戌 Water Dog	Clash: Dragon	Influence:	12 Rulers: Accomplish	Flying star: 5
	Good: Pray, New Construction, Pay Tribute, Opening, Visiting relatives, Sign contract, Gathering, Trading, New school, Herding, Clean house, Sewing, Take Animal, Acupuncture, Build Dam		**Bad**: Move House, Travel, Return Home Land, New Job	

23 Sunday 癸亥 Water Pig	Clash: Snake	Influence: ❶ ❹	12 Rulers: Harvest	Flying star: 6
	Good: Pray, Ritual bath		**Bad**: Burial, Marriage, Break Ground	

24 Monday 甲子 Wood Rat	Clash: Horse	Influence: ❹	12 Rulers: Opening	Flying star: 7
	Good: Pray, Ritual bath, New school		**Bad**: Mitzvah, Marriage, Engagement, Burial	

25 Tuesday 乙丑 Wood Ox	Clash: Goat	Influence: ❹	12 Rulers: Closing	Flying star: 8
	Good: Build Dam, Fix Floor, Fill Hole		**Bad**: Rashly Action	

February

26 Wednesday
丙寅
Fire Tiger

Clash	Monkey
Influence	③
12 Rulers	Establish
Flying star	9

Good: Visiting relatives, Sign contract, Gathering, Engagement, Collect Money, Delivery, Wedding gift, Shipments, Propose marriage, Sewing, Take Animal, Erect pole, Burial, Trading

Bad: Pray, New Job, Marriage, Travel

27 Thursday
丁卯
Fire Rabbit

Clash	Rooster
Influence	③
12 Rulers	Removal
Flying star	1

Good: Pray, Marriage, Move House, Pay Tribute, Cut Nail, Pray for Progeny, Sewing, Visiting relatives, Gathering, New Construction, Travel, Cast Beam, New Job, Engagement, Sign contract

Bad: Hunting, Cut hair, Fishing, Dig Well

28 Friday
戊辰
Earth Dragon

Clash	Dog
Influence	③
12 Rulers	Fulfill
Flying star	2

Good: Pray, Pay Tribute, Policy review, Visiting relatives, Gathering, Sewing, Acupuncture

Bad: Trading, New Job, Sign contract, Marriage

March

1 Saturday
己巳
Earth Snake

Clash	Pig
Influence	
12 Rulers	Balance
Flying star	3

Good: Repair Road

Bad: Think Thrice, Except above

March

2 Sunday 庚午 Metal Horse	Clash Rat	Influence	12 Rulers Stability	Flying star 4
	Good Pray, Marriage, Engagement, Pay Tribute, Sign contract, Receive award, Trading, Visiting relatives, Move House, Gathering, Sewing, Travel, Shipments, New Job, Politics, Burial			Bad Buy House, Repair House, Demolish, Break Ground

3 Monday 辛未 Metal Goat	Clash Ox	Influence	12 Rulers Control	Flying star 5
	Good Pray, Marriage, Engagement, Pay Tribute, New Construction, Receive award, Cast Beam, Policy review, Visiting relatives, Move House, Gathering, Sewing, Travel, Take Animal, New Job, Politics, Burial			Bad Brew Wine, Fishing, Hunting, Recuperate

4 Tuesday 壬申 Water Monkey	Clash Tiger	Influence ❷*	12 Rulers Clash	Flying star 6
	Good Pray, Recuperate, Clean Floor, Clean house, Demolish, Ritual bath, Break Floor, Visit Doctor			Bad Pay Tribute, Marriage, Burial, Trading

5 Wednesday 癸酉 Water Rooster	Clash Rabbit	Influence ❷* ❹*	12 Rulers Accomplish	Flying star 7
	Good Pray, Ritual bath, Cut hair, Cut Nail, Clean Floor, Fishing, Break Ground, Burial			Bad Visiting relatives, Marriage, Gathering, Sign contract, Travel

* 5 MAR- Bomb 2: Valid *after* 16:09
Bomb 4: Valid *after* 16:09

March

6 Thursday 甲戌 Wood Dog				
Clash Dragon	**Influence** ❹		**12 Rulers** Danger	**Flying star** 8
Good Visiting relatives, Pray, Gathering, Pay Tribute, Travel, New Job, Marriage, Move House, Wedding gift, Fix Bed, Repair House, Planting, Opening, Herding, Sign contract, Brew Wine, Burial			**Bad** Sewing, Fishing	

7 Friday 乙亥 Wood Pig				
Clash Snake	**Influence** ❶		**12 Rulers** Accomplish	**Flying star** 9
Good Ritual bath, New school, Visiting relatives, Visit Doctor, Gathering, Sewing, Travel, Build Dam, Move House, Acupuncture, New Construction, Brew Wine, Repair House, Herding, Cast Beam, Erect pole, Take Animal			**Bad** Marriage, Opening, Break Ground, Burial	

8 Saturday 丙子 Fire Rat				
Clash Horse	**Influence**		**12 Rulers** Harvest	**Flying star** 1
Good Be Careful			**Bad** Major Moves	

9 Sunday 丁丑 Fire Ox				
Clash Goat	**Influence**		**12 Rulers** Opening	**Flying star** 2
Good Pray, Wedding gift, Pay Tribute, Marriage, Clean house, Pray for Progeny, Visiting relatives, Repair House, Gathering, New Construction, Travel, Buy House, New Job, Dig Well, Move House, Sewing, Take Animal			**Bad** Cut hair, Opening, Boating, Fishing	

March

10 Monday 戊寅 Earth Tiger	**Clash** Monkey	**Influence** ❸	**12 Rulers** Closing	**Flying star** 3
	Good Sewing, Sign contract, Build Dam, Trading, Fix warehouse, Collect Money, Fix Floor, Herding, Planting, Fill Hole, Acupuncture, Burial			**Bad** Pray, Move House, Clean house, Hunting

11 Tuesday 己卯 Earth Rabbit	**Clash** Rooster	**Influence** ❸	**12 Rulers** Establish	**Flying star** 4
	Good Be Careful			**Bad** Think Thrice

12 Wednesday 庚辰 Metal Dragon	**Clash** Dog	**Influence** ❸	**12 Rulers** Removal	**Flying star** 5
	Good Travel, New Job, Politics, Clean house, Ritual bath, Cut hair, Cut Nail, Clean Floor			**Bad** Marriage, Opening, Burial, Travel

13 Thursday 辛巳 Metal Snake	**Clash** Pig	**Influence**	**12 Rulers** Fulfill	**Flying star** 6
	Good Pray, Pay Tribute, Visiting relatives, Gathering, Sewing, Opening, Sign contract, Trading, Collect Money			**Bad** Travel, Marriage, Buy House, Burial

March

14 Friday 壬午 Water Horse	**Clash** Rat	**Influence**	**12 Rulers** Balance	**Flying star** 7
	Good Pray, Decoration, Paint Wall, Repair Road		**Bad** Pay Tribute, Marriage, Opening, New Construction	

15 Saturday 癸未 Water Goat	**Clash** Ox	**Influence**	**12 Rulers** Stability	**Flying star** 8
	Good Visiting relatives, Gathering, Pest Control		**Bad** Delivery, Opening, Payment, Sign contract	

16 Sunday 甲申 Wood Monkey	**Clash** Tiger	**Influence** ❹	**12 Rulers** Control	**Flying star** 9
	Good Pray, Ritual bath, Clean Floor, Pest Control		**Bad** Trading, Fix Bed, Fishing, Collect Money	

17 Monday 乙酉 Wood Rooster	**Clash** Rabbit	**Influence** ❷ ❹	**12 Rulers** Clash	**Flying star** 1
	Good Demolish, Break Floor		**Bad** Major Moves	

March

18 Tuesday 丙戌 Fire Dog	Clash: Dragon	Influence: ❹	12 Rulers: Danger	Flying star: 2
	Good: Pray, Fishing			Bad: Visit Doctor, Recuperate, Policy review

19 Wednesday 丁亥 Fire Pig	Clash: Snake	Influence: ❶ ❺	12 Rulers: Accomplish	Flying star: 3
	Good: Engagement, Pray, Visiting relatives, Fix warehouse, Gathering, Opening, New school, Sign contract, Travel, Trading, Move House, Collect Money, New Job Shipments, Build Dam			Bad: Burial, Marriage, Cut hair

20 Thursday 戊子 Earth Rat	Clash: Horse	Influence:	12 Rulers: Harvest	Flying star: 4
	Good: Hunting, Fishing			Bad: Opening, Travel

21 Friday 己丑 Earth Ox	Clash: Goat	Influence:	12 Rulers: Opening	Flying star: 5
	Good: Engagement, Pray, Visiting relatives, Marriage, Gathering, Opening, New school, Collect Money, New Job, New Construction, Wedding gift, Cast Beam, Propose marriage, Buy House, Move House, Clean house, Take Animal			Bad: Logging, Fishing, Hunting, Boating

March

22 Saturday 庚寅 Metal Tiger	**Clash** Monkey	**Influence** ❸	**12 Rulers** Closing	**Flying star** 6
	Good Sewing, Fill Hole, Planting, Build Dam, Herding, Brew Wine, Take Animal, Sign contract, Break Ground, Trading, Collect Money		**Bad** Marriage, Travel, Buy House, Opening	

23 Sunday 辛卯 Metal Rabbit	**Clash** Rooster	**Influence** ❸	**12 Rulers** Establish	**Flying star** 7
	Good Pray, Sign contract, Receive award, Trading, Travel, Receive award, Visiting relatives, Gathering, New Job, Politics, New Job		**Bad** Boating, Marriage, Buy House, Burial	

24 Monday 壬辰 Water Dragon	**Clash** Dog	**Influence** ❸	**12 Rulers** Removal	**Flying star** 8
	Good Receive award, Ritual bath, Cut hair, Receive award, Travel, Cut Nail, New Job, Clean Floor, New Job, Clean house, Politics		**Bad** Buy House, Marriage, Burial, Opening	

25 Tuesday 癸巳 Water Snake	**Clash** Pig	**Influence**	**12 Rulers** Fulfill	**Flying star** 9
	Good Pray, Pay Tribute, Visiting relatives, Gathering, Sewing, Acupuncture, Opening, Sign contract, Trading		**Bad** Marriage, Travel, Burial, Move House	

March

26 Wednesday 甲午 Wood Horse	Clash Rat	Influence	12 Rulers Balance	Flying star 1
	Good Pray, Decoration, Paint Wall, Repair Road		Bad Hunting, Fishing, Payment	

27 Thursday 乙未 Wood Goat	Clash Ox	Influence	12 Rulers Stability	Flying star 2
	Good Pray, Pay Tribute, Pray for Progeny, Visiting relatives, Gathering, Sewing, Acupuncture, Brew Wine, Collect Money		Bad Marriage, Move House, Burial, New Construction	

28 Friday 丙申 Fire Monkey	Clash Tiger	Influence ❹	12 Rulers Control	Flying star 3
	Good Pray, Ritual bath, Clean Floor, Pest Control, Fishing		Bad Buy House, Marriage, Burial, Opening	

29 Saturday 丁酉 Fire Rooster	Clash Rabbit	Influence ❷ ❹	12 Rulers Clash	Flying star 4
	Good Demolish, Break Floor		Bad Rashly Action	

March

30 Sunday 戊戌 Earth Dog	Clash Dragon	Influence ❹	12 Rulers Danger	Flying star 5
	Good Fishing			Bad Decoration, Travel, Cut hair, Demolish

31 Monday 己亥 Earth Pig	Clash Snake	Influence ❶	12 Rulers Accomplish	Flying star 6
	Good Engagement, New school, Opening, Travel, Sign contract, New Job, Trading, Move House, Collect Money, Repair House, Take Animal, New Construction, Herding, Cast Beam, Planting, Build Dam			Bad Marriage, Hunting, Fishing

April

1 Tuesday 庚子 Metal Rat	Clash Horse	Influence	12 Rulers Harvest	Flying star 7
	Good Fishing, Pest Control			Bad Delivery, Payment

2 Wednesday 辛丑 Metal Ox	Clash Goat	Influence	12 Rulers Opening	Flying star 8
	Good Pray, Repair House, Pay Tribute, New Construction, Cast Beam, Pray for Progeny, Buy House, New school, Dig Well, Travel, Clean house, Move House, Herding, Visiting relatives, Gathering, Take Animal, New Job			Bad Boating, Opening, Fishing, Sign contract

April

3 Thursday 壬寅 Water Tiger	Clash	Influence	12 Rulers	Flying star
	Monkey	3	Closing	9
	Good			**Bad**
	Sewing, Fill Hole, Planting, Build Dam, Herding, Acupuncture, Brew Wine, Take Animal, Break Ground, Sign contract, Trading, Fix Floor, Collect Money			Marriage, Opening, Buy House, Move House

4 Friday 癸卯 Water Rabbit	Clash	Influence	12 Rulers	Flying star
	Rooster	3 *	Establish	1
	Good			**Bad**
	Visiting relatives, Pray, Gathering, Receive award, Travel, Sign contract, Receive award, Trading, New Job, Politics, New Job			Buy House, Marriage, Burial, New Construction

5 Saturday 甲辰 Wood Dragon	Clash	Influence	12 Rulers	Flying star
	Dog	3 7	Establish	2
	Good			**Bad**
	Pray, Pay Tribute			Opening, Marriage, Move House, New Construction,

6 Sunday 乙巳 Wood Snake	Clash	Influence	12 Rulers	Flying star
	Pig	4 7	Removal	3
	Good			**Bad**
	Ritual bath, Clean Floor			Wedding gift, Fix Bed, Repair House, Break Ground,

* 4 APR- Bomb 3: Valid 24 hours

April

7 Monday 丙午 Fire Horse	Clash Rat	Influence ④	12 Rulers Fulfill	Flying star 4
	Good Pray			Bad Be Conservative

8 Tuesday 丁未 Fire Goat	Clash Ox	Influence ④	12 Rulers Balance	Flying star 5
	Good Pray, Repair Road			Bad Pay Tribute, Travel, Cut hair, Marriage

9 Wednesday 戊申 Earth Monkey	Clash Tiger	Influence	12 Rulers Stability	Flying star 6
	Good Ritual bath, Clean Floor			Bad Be Conservative

10 Thursday 己酉 Earth Rooster	Clash Rabbit	Influence	12 Rulers Control	Flying star 7
	Good Cut hair, Pray, Pay Tribute, Cut Nail, Ritual bath, Marriage, Clean Floor, Clean house, Pest Control, Acupuncture, Brew Wine, Fishing, Take Animal, Visit Doctor, Burial, Recuperate			Bad Visiting relatives, Gathering, Opening, Buy House, Demolish

April

11 Friday
庚戌
Metal Dog

Clash	Influence	12 Rulers	Flying star
Dragon	❷	Clash	8

Good: Pray, Clean house, Ritual bath, Visit Doctor, Recuperate, Demolish, Break Floor

Bad: Travel, Marriage, Boating, Burial

12 Saturday
辛亥
Metal Pig

Clash	Influence	12 Rulers	Flying star
Snake	❶	Danger	9

Good: Visiting relatives, Gathering, Fix Bed, Ritual bath, Collect Money, Fishing, Planting, Herding, Take Animal

Bad: Marriage, Travel, Break Ground, Burial

13 Sunday
壬子
Water Rat

Clash	Influence	12 Rulers	Flying star
Horse		Accomplish	1

Good: Pray, Marriage, Pay Tribute, Wedding gift, Repair House, Pray for Progeny, Visiting relatives, New Construction, Gathering, Opening, New school, Sign contract, Travel, Take Animal, New Job, Burial

Bad: Move House, Fix Sewage, Return Home Land, Fishing

14 Monday
癸丑
Water Ox

Clash	Influence	12 Rulers	Flying star
Goat		Harvest	2

Good: Pray, Adoption, Collect Money, Pest Control, Take Animal

Bad: Marriage, Travel, Burial, Move House

April

15 Tuesday 甲寅 Wood Tiger	Clash: Monkey	Influence: ❸	12 Rulers: Opening	Flying star: 3
	Good Sewing, Policy review, New Construction, Receive award, Visiting relatives, Cast Beam, Gathering, Opening, Travel, Sign contract, Move House, Trading, New Job, Buy House, Politics, Planting, Clean house			**Bad** Engagement, Fishing, Boating, Marriage

16 Wednesday 乙卯 Wood Rabbit	Clash: Rooster	Influence: ❸	12 Rulers: Closing	Flying star: 4
	Good Fix Floor, Fill Hole			**Bad** Marriage, Opening, Burial, Trading

17 Thursday 丙辰 Fire Dragon	Clash: Dog	Influence: ❸	12 Rulers: Establish	Flying star: 5
	Good Pray			**Bad** Marriage, New Construction, Cut hair, Burial

18 Friday 丁巳 Fire Snake	Clash: Pig	Influence: ❹	12 Rulers: Removal	Flying star: 6
	Good Engagement, Pray, Pay Tribute, Marriage, Cut Nail, Pray for Progeny, Sewing, Visiting relatives, Gathering, New Construction, New Job, Opening, Move House, Clean house, Sign contract, Clean Floor, Ritual bath			**Bad** Hunting, Travel, Cut hair, Fishing

April

19 Saturday 戊午 **Earth Horse**	**Clash** Rat	**Influence** ❹	**12 Rulers** Fulfill	**Flying star** 7
	Good Pray		**Bad** Marriage, Opening, Burial, Sign contract	

20 Sunday 己未 **Earth Goat**	**Clash** Ox	**Influence** ❹	**12 Rulers** Balance	**Flying star** 8
	Good Pray, Pay Tribute		**Bad** Major Moves	

21 Monday 庚申 **Metal Monkey**	**Clash** Tiger	**Influence**	**12 Rulers** Stability	**Flying star** 9
	Good Pray, Ritual bath, Clean Floor		**Bad** Marriage, Opening, Burial, Travel	

22 Tuesday 辛酉 **Metal Rooster**	**Clash** Rabbit	**Influence**	**12 Rulers** Control	**Flying star** 1
	Good Pray, Ritual bath, Clean Floor, Cut hair, Cut Nail, Pest Control		**Bad** Marriage, Move House, Buy House, Burial	

April

23 **Wednesday** 壬戌	**Clash** Dragon	**Influence** ❷	**12 Rulers** Clash	**Flying star** 2
	Good Pray, Ritual bath, Clean house, Visit Doctor, Demolish		**Bad** Marriage, Travel, Burial, New Construction	

24 **Thursday** 癸亥 **Water Pig**	**Clash** Snake	**Influence** ❶	**12 Rulers** Danger	**Flying star** 3
	Good Ritual bath		**Bad** Pay Tribute, Marriage, Burial, Fix warehouse	

25 **Friday** 甲子 **Wood Rat**	**Clash** Horse	**Influence**	**12 Rulers** Accomplish	**Flying star** 4
	Good Pray, Ritual bath, Sewing, Pay Tribute, Cast Beam, Receive award, Acupuncture, Visiting relatives, Gathering, Brew Wine, New school, Opening, Travel, Sign contract, New Job, Politics, Trading		**Bad** Marriage, Move House, Burial, Dig Well	

26 **Saturday** 乙丑 **Wood Ox**	**Clash** Goat	**Influence**	**12 Rulers** Harvest	**Flying star** 5
	Good Pray, Adoption, Collect Money, Pest Control, Take Animal, Fishing		**Bad** Engagement, Fix warehouse, Break Ground, Demolish,	

April

27 Sunday 丙寅 Fire Tiger	Clash: Monkey	Influence: ❸	12 Rulers: Opening	Flying star: 6
	Good Engagement, Visiting relatives, Gathering, New Construction, New school, Cast Beam, Travel, Opening, New Job, Sign contract, Move House, Clean house, Trading, Buy House, Sewing			**Bad** Pray, Marriage, Boating, Fishing

28 Monday 丁卯 Fire Rabbit	Clash: Rooster	Influence: ❸	12 Rulers: Closing	Flying star: 7
	Good Pray, Sewing, Fix Floor, Fill Hole			**Bad** Acupuncture, Cut hair, Fishing, Eye care

29 Tuesday 戊辰 Earth Dragon	Clash: Dog	Influence: ❸	12 Rulers: Establish	Flying star: 8
	Good Pray, Pay Tribute			**Bad** Repair House, New Construction

30 Wednesday 己巳 Earth Snake	Clash: Pig	Influence: ❹	12 Rulers: Removal	Flying star: 9
	Good Ritual bath, Clean Floor			**Bad** Pay Tribute, Demolish, Repair House, Fix Bed

May

1 Thursday 庚午 Metal Horse	Clash Rat	Influence ❹	12 Rulers Fulfill	Flying star 1
	Good Pray		Bad Cut Nail, Pray for Progeny	

2 Friday 辛未 Metal Goat	Clash Ox	Influence ❹	12 Rulers Balance	Flying star 2
	Good Pray, Pay Tribute		Bad Think Thrice, Except above	

3 Saturday 壬申 Water Monkey	Clash Tiger	Influence	12 Rulers Stability	Flying star 3
	Good Pray, Ritual bath, Clean Floor		Bad Marriage, Move House, Fishing, Fix Bed	

4 Sunday 癸酉 Water Rooster	Clash Rabbit	Influence ❻	12 Rulers Control	Flying star 4
	Good Engagement, Pray, Pay Tribute, Marriage, Acupuncture, Clean house, Brew Wine, Ritual bath, Clean Floor, Cut hair, Pest Control, Cut Nail, Fishing, Visit Doctor, Burial, Take Animal		Bad Sign contract, Opening, Demolish, Break Ground	

May

5 **Monday** 甲戌 **Wood Dog**	**Clash** Dragon	**Influence** ❷*	**12 Rulers** Clash	**Flying star** 5
	Good Pray, Clean house, Ritual bath, Visit Doctor, Demolish		**Bad** Buy House, Travel, Boating, Opening	

6 **Tuesday** 乙亥 **Wood Pig**	**Clash** Snake	**Influence** ❶ ❷	**12 Rulers** Clash	**Flying star** 6
	Good Pray, Clean house, Ritual bath, Demolish, Break Floor		**Bad** Visiting relatives, Pay Tribute, Gathering, Marriage, Repair House	

7 **Wednesday** 丙子 **Fire Rat**	**Clash** Horse	**Influence**	**12 Rulers** Danger	**Flying star** 7
	Good Pray, Fix Bed, Clean house, Pay Tribute, Visiting relatives, Ritual bath, Gathering, Sewing, Travel, Repair House, New Job, New Construction, Move House, Planting, Cast Beam, Herding, Take Animal		**Bad** Fishing, Wedding gift, Hunting, Marriage	

8 **Thursday** 丁丑 **Fire Ox**	**Clash** Goat	**Influence**	**12 Rulers** Accomplish	**Flying star** 8
	Good Visiting relatives, Wedding gift, Gathering, Visit Doctor, New school, Sewing, Travel, Build Dam, New Job, New Construction, Opening, Cast Beam, Sign contract, Fix warehouse, Trading, Brew Wine, Take Animal		**Bad** Marriage, Move House, Cut hair, Fishing	

* 5 MAY - Bomb 2: Valid **before** 13:59

May

9 **Friday** 戊寅 **Earth Tiger**	**Clash** Monkey	**Influence** ❸ ❹	**12 Rulers** Harvest	**Flying star** 9
	Good Pest Control		**Bad** Think Thrice, Except above	

10 **Saturday** 己卯 **Earth Rabbit**	**Clash** Rooster	**Influence** ❸ ❹	**12 Rulers** Opening	**Flying star** 1
	Good Pray, New school		**Bad** Break Ground, Repair House, Burial, Fishing	

11 **Sunday** 庚辰 **Metal Dragon**	**Clash** Dog	**Influence** ❸ ❹	**12 Rulers** Closing	**Flying star** 2
	Good Pray		**Bad** Major Moves	

12 **Monday** 辛巳 **Metal Snake**	**Clash** Pig	**Influence**	**12 Rulers** Establish	**Flying star** 3
	Good Pray, Wedding gift, Pay Tribute, Marriage, Move House, Pray for Progeny, Clean house, Visiting relatives, Gathering, Visit Doctor, New Job, Sewing, Politics, Herding, Cast Beam, Erect pole, Take Animal		**Bad** Travel, Repair House, Break Ground, Fishing	

May

13 Tuesday 壬午 Water Horse	Clash Rat	Influence	12 Rulers Removal	Flying star 4
	Good Pray, Ritual bath, Cut hair, Pay Tribute, Cut Nail, Receive award, Visit Doctor, Travel, Clean Floor, New Job, Clean house, Break Ground, Visiting relatives, Burial, Gathering		Bad Fix Sewage	

14 Wednesday 癸未 Water Goat	Clash Ox	Influence	12 Rulers Fulfill	Flying star 5
	Good Pray		Bad Think Thrice, Except above	

15 Thursday 甲申 Wood Monkey	Clash Tiger	Influence	12 Rulers Balance	Flying star 6
	Good Pray, Ritual bath, Clean Floor, Repair Road		Bad Pay Tribute, New Construction, Demolish, Fix Bed	

16 Friday 乙酉 Wood Rooster	Clash Rabbit	Influence	12 Rulers Stability	Flying star 7
	Good Engagement, Pray, Pay Tribute, Marriage, New Construction, Pray for Progeny, Buy House, Travel, Opening, New Job, Trading, Move House, Clean Floor, Cut hair, Burial, Cut Nail		Bad Visiting relatives, Fishing, Gathering, Planting, Hunting	

May

17 Saturday 丙戌 Fire Dog	Clash Dragon	Influence	12 Rulers Control	Flying star 8
	Good Pray, Ritual bath, Cut hair, Pay Tribute, Cut Nail, Pray for Progeny, Sewing, Pest Control, Receive award, Visiting relatives, Gathering, Policy review			**Bad** Opening, Travel, New Construction, Move House

18 Sunday 丁亥 Fire Pig	Clash Snake	Influence ❶ ❷	12 Rulers Clash	Flying star 9
	Good Ritual bath, Demolish, Break Floor			**Bad** Buy House, Opening, Marriage, Sign contract

19 Monday 戊子 Earth Rat	Clash Horse	Influence	12 Rulers Danger	Flying star 1
	Good Pray, Ritual bath, Visiting relatives, Gathering, Sewing			**Bad** Trading, Fix Bed, Take Animal, Cast Beam

20 Tuesday 己丑 Earth Ox	Clash Goat	Influence	12 Rulers Accomplish	Flying star 2
	Good Engagement, Pray, Pay Tribute, Repair House, New Construction, Pray for Progeny, Buy House, Travel, Opening, New Job, Trading, New school, Planting, Visiting relatives, Gathering, Clean house, Take Animal			**Bad** Marriage, Move House, Boating, Fishing

May

21 Wednesday 庚寅 Metal Tiger	Clash: Monkey	Influence: ❸ ❹	12 Rulers: Harvest	Flying star: 3
	Good Engagement, Policy review, Marriage, Receive award, Visiting relatives, Cast Beam, Gathering, Sign contract, Travel, Trading, New Job, Pest Control, Move House, Clean house Burial, Sewing			**Bad** Pray, Demolish, Buy House, New Construction

22 Thursday 辛卯 Metal Rabbit	Clash: Rooster	Influence: ❸ ❹	12 Rulers: Opening	Flying star: 4
	Good Engagement, Pray, Pay Tribute, Marriage, New Construction, Pray for Progeny, Buy House, Travel, Opening, New Job, Trading, New school, Planting, Visiting relatives, Gathering, Clean house, Take Animal			**Bad** Brew Wine, Dig Well, Hunting, Logging

23 Friday 壬辰 Water Dragon	Clash: Dog	Influence: ❸ ❹	12 Rulers: Closing	Flying star: 5
	Good Build Dam, Fix Floor, Fill Hole			**Bad** Major Changes

24 Saturday 癸巳 Water Snake	Clash: Pig	Influence:	12 Rulers: Establish	Flying star: 6
	Good Receive award, Receive award, Visiting relatives, Gathering, New Job, Politics, Public relation, Sewing			**Bad** Pay Tribute, Travel, Cut hair, Cut Nail

143

May

25 Sunday 甲午 Wood Horse	**Clash** Rat	**Influence**	**12 Rulers** Removal	**Flying star** 7
	Good Engagement, Pray, Pay Tribute, Marriage, Clean house, Travel, Clean Floor, New Job, New Construction, Move House, Visiting relatives, Repair House, Gathering, Break Ground, Ritual bath		**Bad** Hunting, Fishing, Payment	

26 Monday 乙未 Wood Goat	**Clash** Ox	**Influence**	**12 Rulers** Fulfill	**Flying star** 8
	Good Pray		**Bad** Move House, Travel, Boating, Marriage	

27 Tuesday 丙申 Fire Monkey	**Clash** Tiger	**Influence**	**12 Rulers** Balance	**Flying star** 9
	Good Engagement, Pray, Visiting relatives, Marriage, Gathering, Acupuncture, Travel, Brew Wine, New Job, Opening, Move House, Sign contract, Ritual bath, New Construction, Cut Nail, Cut hair, Repair House		**Bad** Good for Everything	

28 Wednesday 丁酉 Fire Rooster	**Clash** Rabbit	**Influence**	**12 Rulers** Stability	**Flying star** 1
	Good Engagement, Travel, Marriage, New Job, Cast Beam, Wedding gift, New Construction, Propose marriage, Opening, Move House, Trading, Ritual bath, Break Ground, Cut Nail, Acupuncture, Burial		**Bad** Cut hair, Visiting relatives, Gathering, Buy House, Clean house	

May

29 Thursday 戊戌 Earth Dog	Clash	Influence	12 Rulers	Flying star
	Dragon		Control	2
	Good		**Bad**	
	Cut hair, Pray, Pay Tribute, Cut Nail, Sewing, Pray for Progeny, Visiting relatives, Repair House, Gathering, New Construction, New Job, Cast Beam, Move House, Pest Control, Clean house, Planting, Ritual bath		Trading, Travel, Sign contract, Opening	

30 Friday 己亥 Earth Pig	Clash	Influence	12 Rulers	Flying star
	Snake	❶ ❷	Clash	3
	Good		**Bad**	
	Pray, Ritual bath, Clean house, Demolish, Break Floor		Marriage, Repair House, Buy House, Trading	

31 Saturday 庚子 Metal Rat	Clash	Influence	12 Rulers	Flying star
	Horse		Danger	4
	Good		**Bad**	
	Engagement, Pray, Pay Tribute, Marriage, Clean house, Pray for Progeny, Visiting relatives, Ritual bath, Gathering, New Construction, Travel, Fix warehouse, New Job, Break Ground, Move House, Burial, Fix Bed		Hunting, Acupuncture Fishing, Visit Doctor	

June

1 Sunday 辛丑 Metal Ox	Clash	Influence	12 Rulers	Flying star
	Goat		Accomplish	5
	Good		**Bad**	
	Engagement, Pray, Pay Tribute, Marriage, Clean house, Pray for Progeny, Visiting relatives, Opening, Gathering, New Construction, Travel, Fix warehouse, New Job, Sign contract, New school, Sewing, Burial		Brew Wine, Move House, Return Home Land, Fishing	

June

2 Monday 壬寅 Water Tiger	Clash Monkey	Influence 3 ✦ 4 ✦	12 Rulers Harvest	Flying star 6
	Good Pest Control		Bad Marriage, Trading, Burial, Move House	

3 Tuesday 癸卯 Water Rabbit	Clash Rooster	Influence 3 ✦ 4 ✦	12 Rulers Opening	Flying star 7
	Good Pray, New school		Bad Acupuncture, Dig Well, Brew Wine, Logging	

4 Wednes- day 甲辰 Wood	Clash Dog	Influence 3 ✦ 7 ✦ 4 ✦	12 Rulers Closing	Flying star 8
	Good Build Dam, Fill Hole, Fix Floor		Bad Think Thrice, Except above	

5 Thursday 乙巳 Wood Snake	Clash Pig	Influence 7 ✦ *	12 Rulers Establish	Flying star 9
	Good Engagement, Pray, Pay Tribute, Marriage, Clean house, Pray for Progeny, Sewing, Visiting relatives, Gathering, Erect pole, New Job, Cast Beam, Wedding gift, Herding, Propose marriage, Take Animal, Move House			Bad Buy House, Travel, Decoration, New Construction

*5 JUN – Bomb 7: Valid 24 hours

June

6 Friday 丙午 Fire Horse	**Clash** Rat	**Influence**	**12 Rulers** Establish	**Flying star** 1
	Good Be Careful		**Bad** Be Patient	

7 Saturday 丁未 Fire Goat	**Clash** Ox	**Influence**	**12 Rulers** Removal	**Flying star** 2
	Good Gathering, New school, Travel, New Job, Marriage, Visiting relatives, Pray, Gathering, Pay Tribute, Travel, New Job, Pray for Progeny, Move House, Wedding gift, Repair House, Marriage, Cut Nail, New Construction, Acupuncture, Opening, Brew Wine, Sign contract		**Bad** Cut hair, Visit Doctor, Recuperate	

8 Sunday 戊申 Earth Monkey	**Clash** Tiger	**Influence**	**12 Rulers** Fulfill	**Flying star** 3
	Good Cut hair, Pray, Pay Tribute, Ritual bath, Cut Nail, Pray for Progeny, Clean house, Travel, Cast Beam, New Job, Repair House, Opening, New Construction, Marriage, Fix Floor, Planting		**Bad** Visiting relatives, Wedding gift, Gathering, Fix Bed, Sign contract	

9 Monday 己酉 Earth Rooster	**Clash** Rabbit	**Influence**	**12 Rulers** Balance	**Flying star** 4
	Good Pray, Ritual bath, Cut hair, Cut Nail, Clean Floor, Paint Wall, Repair Road		**Bad** Travel, Marriage, Opening, Burial	

June

10 **Tuesday** 庚戌 **Metal Dog**	**Clash** Dragon	**Influence**	**12 Rulers** Stability	**Flying star** 5
	Good Pray, Wedding gift, Pay Tribute, Marriage, Sewing, Visiting relatives, Gathering, Mitzvah, Repair House, New Construction, New Job, Erect pole, Sign contract, Fix warehouse, Trading, Brew Wine, Take Animal		**Bad** Clean house, Acupuncture, Buy House, Planting	

11 **Wednesday** 辛亥 **Metal Pig**	**Clash** Snake	**Influence** ❶ ❹	**12 Rulers** Control	**Flying star** 6
	Good Pray, Ritual bath, Pest Control		**Bad** Marriage, Opening, Sign contract, Fishing	

12 **Thursday** 壬子 **Water Rat**	**Clash** Horse	**Influence** ❷ ❹	**12 Rulers** Clash	**Flying star** 7
	Good Be Careful		**Bad** Rashly Action	

13 **Friday** 癸丑 **Water Ox**	**Clash** Goat	**Influence** ❹	**12 Rulers** Danger	**Flying star** 8
	Good Pray		**Bad** Major Moves	

June

14 Saturday 甲寅 Wood Tiger	Clash: Monkey	Influence: ❸	12 Rulers: Accomplish	Flying star: 9
	Good Visiting relatives, Opening, Gathering, Sign contract, New school, Collect Money, New Job, Brew Wine, Build Dam, Sewing, Repair House, New Construction, Take Animal, Herding, Break Ground, Planting, Burial			**Bad** Pray, Wedding gift, Marriage, Move House

15 Sunday 乙卯 Wood Rabbit	Clash: Rooster	Influence: ❸	12 Rulers: Harvest	Flying star: 1
	Good Pray			**Bad** Visiting relatives, Opening, Gathering, Burial, Marriage

16 Monday 丙辰 Fire Dragon	Clash: Dog	Influence: ❸	12 Rulers: Opening	Flying star: 2
	Good Engagement, Pray, Pay Tribute, Marriage, Opening, Pray for Progeny, Buy House, Visiting relatives, Gathering, New Construction, Travel, Repair House, New Job, Dig Well, New school, Fix warehouse, Move House			**Bad** Logging, Hunting, Fishing

17 Tuesday 丁巳 Fire Snake	Clash: Pig	Influence:	12 Rulers: Closing	Flying star: 3
	Good Sewing, Build Dam, Fix Floor, Fill Hole			**Bad** Pay Tribute, Marriage, Burial, Move House

149

June

18 Wednesday 戊午 Earth Horse	Clash Rat	Influence	12 Rulers Establish	Flying star 4
	Good Pray			Bad Repair House, New Construction

19 Thursday 己未 Earth Goat	Clash Ox	Influence	12 Rulers Removal	Flying star 5
	Good Opening, Gathering, Sign contract, New school, Collect Money, New Job, Brew Wine, Build Dam, Sewing, Repair House, New Construction, Take Animal, Herding, Break Ground, Planting, Burial			Bad Engagement, Wedding gift, Propose marriage, Marriage

20 Friday 庚申 Metal Monkey	Clash Tiger	Influence ❺	12 Rulers Fulfill	Flying star 6
	Good Sewing, Pray, Pay Tribute, Opening, Collect Money, Travel, Fix Floor, Move House, Clean house, Fill Hole, Clean Floor, Ritual bath, Cut hair, Break Ground, Burial, Cut Nail			Bad Visiting relatives, Marriage, Gathering, Sign contract, Fix Bed

21 Saturday 辛酉 Metal Rooster	Clash Rabbit	Influence	12 Rulers Balance	Flying star 7
	Good Pray, Ritual bath, Cut hair, Cut Nail, Clean Floor, Decoration, Repair Road			Bad Hunting, Travel, Visiting relatives, Fishing, Gathering

June

22 Sunday 壬戌 Water Dog	Clash	Influence	12 Rulers	Flying star
	Dragon		Stability	8
	Good			**Bad**
	Engagement, Pray, Pay Tribute, Marriage, Erect pole, Policy review, Visiting relatives, Cast Beam, Gathering, Acupuncture Mitzvah, Sign contract, New Job, Sewing, Trading, Brew Wine, Collect Money			Buy House, Clean house, Demolish, Repair House

23 Monday 癸亥 Water Pig	Clash	Influence	12 Rulers	Flying star
	Snake	❶ ❹	Control	9
	Good			**Bad**
	Pray, Ritual bath			Opening, Pray for Progeny, Burial, Marriage

24 Tuesday 甲子 Wood Rat	Clash	Influence	12 Rulers	Flying star
	Horse	❷ ❹	Clash	9
	Good			**Bad**
	Pray			Major Moves

25 Wednesday 乙丑 Wood Ox	Clash	Influence	12 Rulers	Flying star
	Goat	❹	Danger	8
	Good			**Bad**
	Pray			Rashly Action

June

26 Thursday 丙寅 Fire Tiger	Clash Monkey	Influence ③		12 Rulers Accomplish	Flying star 7
	Good			Bad	
	Engagement, Visiting relatives, Marriage, Gathering, Fix warehouse, New school, Acupuncture, Travel, Opening, New Job, Clean house, Sign contract, Break Ground, Break Ground, Burial, Repair House			Return Home Land, Pray, Fishing, Move House	

27 Friday 丁卯 Fire Rabbit	Clash Rooster	Influence ③		12 Rulers Harvest	Flying star 6
	Good			Bad	
	Pray			Marriage, Travel, Burial, Move House	

28 Saturday 戊辰 Earth Dragon	Clash Dog	Influence ③		12 Rulers Opening	Flying star 5
	Good			Bad	
	Engagement, Pray, Pay Tribute, New Construction, Cast Beam, Pray for Progeny, Buy House, New school, Dig Well, Travel, Clean house, Move House, Herding, Visiting relatives, Gathering, Take Animal, New Job			Fix warehouse, Opening, Logging, Fishing	

29 Sunday 己巳 Earth Snake	Clash Pig	Influence		12 Rulers Closing	Flying star 4
	Good			Bad	
	Pray, Sewing, Build Dam, Collect Money, Fix Floor, Fill Hole, Planting, Herding			Marriage, Opening, Burial, Move House	

June

30 Monday 庚午 Metal Horse	Clash: Rat	Influence:	12 Rulers: Closing	Flying star: 3
	Good: Pray		Bad: Repair House, New Construction	

July

1 Tuesday 辛未 Metal Goat	Clash: Ox	Influence:	12 Rulers: Removal	Flying star: 2
	Good: Engagement, Pray, Pay Tribute, Marriage, Fix warehouse, New school, Acupuncture, Travel, Visiting relatives, Gathering, New Job, Clean house, Sign contract, Move House, New Construction, Burial, Repair House		Bad: Brew Wine, Fishing, Hunting, Visit Doctor	

2 Wednesday 壬申 Water Monkey	Clash: Tiger	Influence:	12 Rulers: Fulfill	Flying star: 1
	Good: Pray, Opening, Pay Tribute, Collect Money, Fix Floor, Fill Hole, Travel, Clean Floor, Move House, Clean house, Break Ground, Burial, Cut Nail, Acupuncture Cut hair,		Bad: Visiting relatives, Fix bed, Gathering, Fix Sewage, Sign Contract	

3 Thursday 癸酉 Water Rooster	Clash: Rabbit	Influence:	12 Rulers: Balance	Flying star: 9
	Good: Ritual bath, Cut hair, Cut Nail, Clean Floor, Decoration, Paint Wall, Repair Road		Bad: Payment, Opening, Marriage	

153

July

4 **Friday** 甲戌 **Wood Dog**	**Clash** Dragon	**Influence**		**12 Rulers** Stability	**Flying star** 8
	Good Engagement, Pray, Pay Tribute, Marriage, Visiting relatives, Repair House, Gathering, New Construction, Policy review, Trading, New Job, Sewing, Sign contract, Adoption					**Bad** Clean house, Buy House, Planting

5 **Saturday** 乙亥 **Wood Pig**	**Clash** Snake	**Influence** ❶ ❹		**12 Rulers** Control	**Flying star** 7
	Good Pray, Ritual bath, Pest Control					**Bad** Marriage, Move House, Burial, Opening

6 **Sunday** 丙子 **Fire Rat**	**Clash** Horse	**Influence** ❷ ❹		**12 Rulers** Clash	**Flying star** 6
	Good Pray, Ritual bath					**Bad** Marriage, Sign contract, Fix Bed, Opening

7 **Monday** 丁丑 **Fire Ox**	**Clash** Goat	**Influence** ❷* ❹*		**12 Rulers** Clash	**Flying star** 5
	Good Be Careful					**Bad** Major Changes

*7 JULY - Bomb 2: Valid **after** 04.06
Bomb 4: Valid **before** 04.06

July

8 Tuesday
戊寅
Earth Tiger

Clash	Influence	12 Rulers	Flying star
Monkey	☯	Danger	4

Good: Visiting relatives, Wedding gift, Gathering, Propose marriage, Travel, Fix Bed, Move House, Sewing, New Job, Repair House, Opening, New Construction, Sign contract, Cast Beam, Delivery, Planting, Payment

Bad: Pray, Pray for Progeny, Clean house, Pay Tribute

9 Wednesday
己卯
Earth Rabbit

Clash	Influence	12 Rulers	Flying star
Rooster	☯	Accomplish	3

Good: Visiting relatives, Pray, Gathering, Pay Tribute, Travel, New school, Marriage, New Job, Wedding gift, Move House, New Construction, Clean house, Opening, Brew Wine, Take Animal, Planting, Sewing

Bad: Dig Well, Hunting, Fishing

10 Thursday
庚辰
Metal Dragon

Clash	Influence	12 Rulers	Flying star
Dog	☯	Harvest	2

Good: Pray, Adoption, Collect Money, Pest Control, Planting, Take Animal

Bad: Move House, Fix Bed, Burial, Marriage

11 Friday
辛巳
Metal Snake

Clash	Influence	12 Rulers	Flying star
Pig		Opening	1

Good: Pray, New school

Bad: Buy House, Cut Nail

July

12 Saturday
壬午
Water Horse

Clash	Influence	12 Rulers	Flying star
Rat		Closing	9

Good	Bad
Acupuncture, Brew Wine, Fix Floor, Fill Hole,| Break Ground, Burial	Marriage, Fix Bed, Sign contract, Fishing

13 Sunday
癸未
Water Goat

Clash	Influence	12 Rulers	Flying star
Ox		Establish	8

Good	Bad
Pray, Receive award, Visiting relatives, Gathering, Travel, New Job, Politics, Marriage	Pay Tribute, Cut hair, Cut hair, Buy House, Burial

14 Monday
甲申
Wood Monkey

Clash	Influence	12 Rulers	Flying star
Tiger	❹	Removal	7

Good	Bad
Pray, Wedding gift, Pay Tribute, Marriage, Clean house, Pray for Progeny, Cut hair, Visiting relatives, Gathering, Cut Nail, New Job, New Construction, Move House, Cast Beam, Take Animal, Break Ground, Burial	Travel, Fix Bed, Fix warehouse, Fishing

15 Tuesday
乙酉
Wood Rooster

Clash	Influence	12 Rulers	Flying star
Rabbit	❹	Fulfill	6

Good	Bad
Pray, Ritual bath, Clean Floor	Marriage, Travel, Opening, Burial

July

16 Wednesday 丙戌 Fire Dog	Clash	Influence	12 Rulers	Flying star
	Dragon	❹	Balance	5
	Good Be Careful		**Bad** Be Conservative	

17 Thursday 丁亥 Fire Pig	Clash	Influence	12 Rulers	Flying star
	Snake	❶	Stability	4
	Good Erect pole, Visiting relatives, Gathering, Mitzvah, Cast Beam, Acupuncture, Politics, Brew Wine, Public relation, Herding, Ritual bath, Sewing, Take Animal		**Bad** Opening, Marriage, Cut hair, Burial	

18 Friday 戊子 Earth Rat	Clash	Influence	12 Rulers	Flying star
	Horse		Control	3
	Good Pray, Ritual bath, Clean Floor, Cut hair, Cut Nail, Pest Control		**Bad** Marriage, Travel, Return Home Land, Burial	

19 Saturday 己丑 Earth Ox	Clash	Influence	12 Rulers	Flying star
	Goat	❷	Clash	2
	Good Pray		**Bad** Marriage, Sign contract, Buy House, Repair House	

July

20 Sunday 庚寅 Metal Tiger				
	Clash Monkey	**Influence** ❸	**12 Rulers** Danger	**Flying star** 1
	Good Engagement, Policy review, Visiting relatives, Delivery, Gathering, Shipments, Fix Bed, Planting, Brew Wine, Herding, Opening, Take Animal, Sign contract, Break Ground, Trading, Collect Money		**Bad** Clean house, Pray, Acupuncture, Pay Tribute	

21 Sunday 辛卯 Metal Rabbit				
	Clash Rooster	**Influence** ❸	**12 Rulers** Accomplish	**Flying star** 9
	Good Engagement, Pray, Pay Tribute, Marriage, New Construction, Pray for Progeny, Visiting relatives, Opening, Gathering, Sign contract, New school, Planting, Travel, Break Ground, New Job, Move House		**Bad** Brew Wine, Dig Well	

22 Tuesday 壬辰 Water Dragon				
	Clash Dog	**Influence** ❸	**12 Rulers** Harvest	**Flying star** 8
	Good Pray, Collect Money, Pest Control, Planting, Herding, Take Animal, Adoption		**Bad** Opening, Move House, Buy House, Marriage	

23 Wednesday 癸巳 Water Snake				
	Clash Pig	**Influence**	**12 Rulers** Opening	**Flying star** 7
	Good Pray, New school		**Bad** Sign contract, Travel, Demolish, Repair House	

July

24 Thursday 甲午 Wood Horse				
Clash Rat	**Influence**	**12 Rulers** Closing	**Flying star** 6	
Good Pray, Sewing, Acupuncture, Brew Wine, Fix Floor, Fill Hole, Break Ground, Burial			**Bad** Political Announcement, Send Troops, Recruiting, Recuperate	

25 Friday 乙未 Wood Goat				
Clash Ox	**Influence**	**12 Rulers** Establish	**Flying star** 5	
Good Pray, Receive award, Receive award, Travel, New Job, Politics, Public relation, Marriage			**Bad** Buy House, Engagement, Burial, New Construction	

26 Saturday 丙申 Fire Monkey				
Clash Rabbit	**Influence** ❹	**12 Rulers** Removal	**Flying star** 4	
Good Pray, Ritual bath, Clean Floor			**Bad** Visiting relatives, Marriage, Gathering, Opening, Travel	

27 Sunday 丁酉 Fire Rooster				
Clash Rabbit	**Influence** ❹	**12 Rulers** Fulfill	**Flying star** 3	
Good Pray, Ritual bath, Clean Floor			**Bad** Marriage, Sign contract, Burial, Move House	

July

28 Monday 戊戌 Earth Dog	Clash Dragon	Influence ❹	12 Rulers Balance	Flying star 2
	Good Pray		Bad Brew Wine, Dig Well	

29 Tuesday 己亥 Earth Pig	Clash Snake	Influence ❶	12 Rulers Stability	Flying star 1
	Good Engagement, Pray, Pay Tribute, Wedding gift, Visiting relatives, New Construction, Gathering, Mitzvah, Repair House, Sign contract, Travel, Trading, New Job, Take Animal, Move House, Planting, Clean house			Bad Hunting, Marriage, Visit Doctor, Fishing

30 Wednesday 庚子 Metal Rat	Clash Horse	Influence	12 Rulers Control	Flying star 9
	Good Ritual bath, Cut hair, Cut Nail, Pest Control			Bad Marriage, Move House, Return Home Land, Burial

31 Wednesday 辛丑	Clash Goat	Influence ❷	12 Rulers Clash	Flying star 8
	Good Be Careful			Bad Big Changes

August

1 Friday 壬寅 Water Tiger	Clash	Influence	12 Rulers	Flying star
	Monkey	③	Danger	7
	Good			Bad
	Visiting relatives, Delivery, Gathering, Shipments, Fix Bed, Planting, Acupuncture, Herding, Brew Wine, Take Animal, Opening, Break Ground, Sign contract, Trading, Engagement, Collect Money			Pray, Fix Sewage, Clean house, Pay Tribute

2 Saturday 癸卯 Water Rabbit	Clash	Influence	12 Rulers	Flying star
	Rooster	③	Accomplish	6
	Good			Bad
	Engagement, Visiting relatives, Gathering, Marriage, New school, Repair House, Travel, New Construction, New Job, Opening, Move House, Sewing, Sign contract, Adoption			Dig Well

3 Sunday 甲辰 Wood Dragon	Clash	Influence	12 Rulers	Flying star
	Dog	③ ⑦	Harvest	5
	Good			Bad
	Engagement, Pray, Pay Tribute, Marriage, Repair House, Pray for Progeny, Visiting relatives, New Construction, Gathering, Collect Money, Travel, Pest Control, New Job, Take Animal, Move House, Clean house, Burial			Hunting, Delivery, Fishing, Payment

4 Monday 乙巳 Wood Snake	Clash	Influence	12 Rulers	Flying star
	Pig	⑦	Opening	4
	Good			Bad
	Pray, New school			Marriage, Sign contract, Burial, Move House

August

5 **Tuesday** 丙午 **Fire Horse**	Clash Rat	Influence	12 Rulers Closing	Flying star 3
	Good Banquet, Brew Wine, Break Ground, Burial			**Bad** Travel, Acupuncture, Dig Well

6 **Wednesday** 丁未 **Fire Goat**	Clash Ox	Influence **6**	12 Rulers Establish	Flying star 2
	Good Pray, Receive award, Receive award, Travel, New Job, New Job, Politics, Public relation			**Bad** Cut hair, Marriage, Burial, Cut Nail

7 **Thursday** 戊申 **Earth Monkey**	Clash Tiger	Influence **4**	12 Rulers Removal	Flying star 1
	Good Pray, Ritual bath, Clean Floor			**Bad** Engagement, Visiting relatives, Gathering, Burial, Sign contract

8 **Friday** 己酉 **Earth Rooster**	Clash Rabbit	Influence	12 Rulers Removal	Flying star 9
	Good Clean house, Ritual bath, Cut hair, Cut Nail, Clean Floor, Break Ground, Burial			**Bad** Marriage, Move House, Cut hair, Burial

August

9 Saturday 庚戌 Metal Dog				
	Clash Dragon	**Influence**	**12 Rulers** Fulfill	**Flying star** 8
	Good Policy Review, Visiting relatives, Gathering, Sewing, Fix Floor, Fill Hole, Planting, Herding, Take Animal,		**Bad** Opening, Marriage, Fishing, Burial	

10 Sunday 辛亥 Metal Pig				
	Clash Snake	**Influence** ❶	**12 Rulers** Balance	**Flying star** 7
	Good Pray, Ritual bath, Decoration, Paint Wall, Repair Road		**Bad** Travel, Marriage, Burial, Opening	

11 Monday 壬子 Water Rat				
	Clash Horse	**Influence**	**12 Rulers** Stability	**Flying star** 6
	Good Pray, Marriage, Pay Tribute, Wedding gift, Repair House, Pray for Progeny, Visiting relatives, New Construction, Gathering, Clean house, Travel, Take Animal, Opening, Break Ground, Sign contract		**Bad** Recuperate, Fix Sewage, Hunting, Fishing,	

12 Tuesday 癸丑 Water Ox				
	Clash Goat	**Influence**	**12 Rulers** Control	**Flying star** 5
	Good Pray, Visit Doctor, Sewing, Pay Tribute, Repair House, Pray for Progeny, Visiting relatives, New Construction, Gathering, Fix warehouse, Travel, Pest Control, New Job, Planting, Take Animal, Clean house, Burial		**Bad** Marriage, Move House, Boating, Hunting	

August

13 Wednesday 甲寅 Wood Tiger	Clash Monkey	Influence ❷ ❸	12 Rulers Clash	Flying star 4
	Good Be Careful			Bad Rashly Action

14 Thursday 乙卯 Wood Rabbit	Clash Rooster	Influence ❸	12 Rulers Danger	Flying star 3
	Good Be Careful			Bad Major Moves

15 Friday 丙辰 Fire Dragon	Clash Dog	Influence ❸	12 Rulers Accomplish	Flying star 2
	Good Pray, New school			Bad Think Thrice, Except above

16 Saturday 丁巳 Fire Snake	Clash Pig	Influence ❹	12 Rulers Harvest	Flying star 1
	Good Pray, Marriage, Pay Tribute, Wedding gift, Clean house, Visiting relatives, Gathering, Cast Beam, Move House, Sewing, Opening, Take Animal, Sign contract, Herding, Trading, Acupuncture, Brew Wine			Bad Cut hair, Travel, Buy House, New Construction

August

17 **Sunday** 戊午 **Earth Horse**	**Clash** Rat	**Influence** ❹	**12 Rulers** Opening	**Flying star** 9
	Good Engagement, Pray, Pay Tribute, Repair House, New Construction, Pray for Progeny, Buy House, Travel, Opening, New Job, Trading, New school, Planting, Visiting relatives, Gathering			**Bad** Logging, Hunting, Fishing

18 **Monday** 己未 **Earth Goat**	**Clash** Ox	**Influence** ❹	**12 Rulers** Closing	**Flying star** 8
	Good Fix Floor, Fill Hole, Build Dam			**Bad** Banquet

19 **Tuesday** 庚申 **Metal Monkey**	**Clash** Tiger	**Influence**	**12 Rulers** Establish	**Flying star** 7
	Good Sewing, Receive award, Collect Money, Receive award, Take Animal, Travel, Politics, New Job, Public relation, New Job, Take Animal, Ritual bath, Clean Floor, Adoption			**Bad** Opening, Fix Bed, Burial, Marriage

20 **Wednesday** 辛酉 **Metal Rooster**	**Clash** Rabbit	**Influence**	**12 Rulers** Removal	**Flying star** 6
	Good Clean house, Ritual bath, Clean Floor, Cut hair, Cut Nail, Break Ground, Burial			**Bad** Boating, Move House, Marriage, Travel

August

21 **Thursday** 壬戌 **Water Dog**	**Clash** Dragon	**Influence**	**12 Rulers** Fulfill	**Flying star** 5
	Good Engagement, Marriage, Receive award, Clean house, Travel, Visiting relatives, Opening, Gathering, Sign contract, New Job, Cast Beam, Wedding gift, New Construction, Propose marriage, Repair House, Move House			**Bad** Hunting, Pray, Fishing, Fix Sewage

22 **Friday** 癸亥 **Water Pig**	**Clash** Snake	**Influence** ❶	**12 Rulers** Balance	**Flying star** 4
	Good Pray, Ritual bath, Decoration, Paint Wall, Repair Road			**Bad** Clean house, Pay Tribute, Fishing, Marriage

23 **Saturday** 甲子 **Wood Rat**	**Clash** Horse	**Influence**	**12 Rulers** Stability	**Flying star** 3
	Good Engagement, Pray, Pay Tribute, Marriage, Opening, Pray for Progeny, Visiting relatives, Sign contract, Gathering, Acupuncture, New Job, Brew Wine, Travel, Herding, Mitzvah, Take Animal, Move House			**Bad** Buy House, Clean house, Planting, Payment

24 **Sunday** 乙丑 **Wood Ox**	**Clash** Goat	**Influence**	**12 Rulers** Control	**Flying star** 2
	Good Visiting relatives, Gathering, Herding, Take Animal, Pest Control			**Bad** Return Home Land, Mitzvah, Opening, Move House

August

25 Monday 丙寅 Fire Tiger	Clash Monkey	Influence ❷ ❸	12 Rulers Clash	Flying star 1
	Good Demolish, Break Floor		Bad Think Thrice, Except above	

26 Tuesday 丁卯 Fire Rabbit	Clash Rooster	Influence ❸	12 Rulers Danger	Flying star 9
	Good Engagement, Pray, Pay Tribute, Marriage, Clean house, Pray for Progeny, Visiting relatives, Sign contract, Gathering, Trading, Travel, Take Animal, New Job, Move House, Burial, Fix Bed		Bad Cut hair, Demolish, Fix Floor, New Construction.	

27 Wednesday 戊辰 Earth Dragon	Clash Dog	Influence ❸	12 Rulers Accomplish	Flying star 8
	Good Pray, Take Animal, Brew Wine, Pay Tribute, Clean house, Pray for Progeny, Visiting relatives, Opening, Gathering, New Construction, Build Dam, Delivery, Cast Beam, Sign contract, New school, Sewing, Burial		Bad Marriage, Travel, Move House, New Job	

28 Thursday 己巳 Earth Snake	Clash Pig	Influence ❹	12 Rulers Harvest	Flying star 7
	Good Engagement, Pray, Pay Tribute, Marriage, Opening, Pray for Progeny, Visiting relatives, Sign contract, Gathering, New Construction, New Job, Repair House, Move House, Acupuncture, Sewing, Brew Wine, Planting		Bad Travel, Recuperate	

August

29 Friday 庚午 Metal Horse	Clash Rat	Influence ④	12 Rulers Opening	Flying star 6
	Good Pray, New school			Bad Mitzvah, Marriage, Burial

30 Saturday 辛未 Metal Goat	Clash Ox	Influence ④	12 Rulers Closing	Flying star 5
	Good Fix Floor, Fill Hole, Build Dam			Bad Banquet

31 Sunday 壬申 Water Monkey	Clash Tiger	Influence	12 Rulers Establish	Flying star 4
	Good Engagement, Pray, Pay Tribute, Marriage, Wedding gift, New Job, Visiting relatives, Repair House, Gathering, Cut Nail, Travel, Cast Beam, Move House, Take Animal, Ritual bath, Cut hair, Burial			Bad New Construction, Fix Bed, Buy House, Repair House

September

1 Monday 癸酉 Water Rooster	Clash Rabbit	Influence	12 Rulers Removal	Flying star 3
	Good Engagement, Pray, Pay Tribute, New Construction, Clean house, Repair House, Collect Money, Ritual bath, Cut hair, Take Animal, Fix warehouse, Cut Nail, Sewing, Break Ground, Clean Floor, Burial			Bad Boating, Marriage, Fishing, Travel

September

2 **Tuesday** 甲戌 **Wood Dog**	**Clash** Dragon	**Influence**	**12 Rulers** Fulfill	**Flying star** 2
	Good Fix Floor, Fill Hole, Receive award, Planting, Sewing, Herding, Take Animal, Visiting relatives, Policy review, Gathering, Acupuncture			**Bad** Pray, Marriage, Sign contract, Opening

3 **Wednesday** 乙亥 **Wood Pig**	**Clash** Snake	**Influence** ❶	**12 Rulers** Balance	**Flying star** 1
	Good Pray, Ritual bath, Fix Floor, Fill Hole, Repair Road			**Bad** Buy House, Marriage, Burial, Move House

4 **Thursday** 丙子 **Fire Rat**	**Clash** Horse	**Influence**	**12 Rulers** Stability	**Flying star** 9
	Good Engagement, Pray, Pay Tribute, Marriage, Opening, Pray for Progeny, Visiting relatives, Sign contract, Gathering, New Construction, Travel, Fix warehouse, New Job, Break Ground, Move House, Brew Wine			**Bad** Boating, Buy House, Clean house, Fishing

5 **Friday** 丁丑 **Fire Ox**	**Clash** Goat	**Influence**	**12 Rulers** Control	**Flying star** 8
	Good Engagement, Pray, Pay Tribute, Marriage, Erect pole, Pray for Progeny, Visiting relatives, Cast Beam, Gathering, New Construction, Travel, Fix warehouse, New Job, Break Ground, Move House, Sewing, Burial			**Bad** Mitzvah, Move House, Return Home Land, Cut hair

September

6 **Saturday** 戊寅 **Earth Tiger**	Clash Monkey	Influence ❷ ❸		12 Rulers Clash	Flying star 7
	Good Ritual bath			Bad Think Thrice, Except above	

7 **Sunday** 己卯 **Earth Rabbit**	Clash Rooster	Influence ❷ * ❸ ❹ *	12 Rulers Accomplish	Flying star 6
	Good Pray, Visiting relatives, Gathering		Bad Travel, Marriage, Burial, Sign contract	

8 **Monday** 庚辰 **Metal Dragon**	Clash Dog	Influence ❸ ❹	12 Rulers Danger	Flying star 5
	Good Visiting relatives, Pray, Gathering, Pay Tribute, Travel, New Job, Pray for Progeny, Move House, Wedding gift, Fix Bed, Marriage, Repair House, Opening, New Construction, Sign contract, Clean house, Burial		Bad Fix warehouse, Delivery, Send Troops, Shipments	

9 **Tuesday** 辛巳 **Metal Snake**	Clash Pig	Influence	12 Rulers Accomplish	Flying star 4
	Good Pray, Wedding gift, Pay Tribute, Marriage, Sewing, Visiting relatives, Gathering, Build Dam, New Job, Repair House, New school, New Construction, Opening, Take Animal, Sign contract, Planting, Trading		Bad Travel, Break Ground, Burial	

* 7 SEPT- Bomb 2: Valid **after** 16.53
Bomb 4: Valid **after** 16.53

September

10 Wednesday 壬午 Water Horse	**Clash** Rat	**Influence**	**12 Rulers** Harvest	**Flying star** 3
	Good Pray, Pest Control		**Bad** Major Changes	

11 Thursday 癸未 Water Goat	**Clash** Ox	**Influence**	**12 Rulers** Opening	**Flying star** 2
	Good Pray, Marriage, Pay Tribute, Wedding gift, Clean house, Pray for Progeny, Sewing, Visiting relatives, Gathering, Erect pole, New school, Cast Beam, Travel, Take Animal, New Job, Herding, Receive award		**Bad** Opening, New Construction, Boating, Sign contract	

12 Friday 甲申 Wood Monkey	**Clash** Tiger	**Influence**	**12 Rulers** Closing	**Flying star** 1
	Good Sewing, Pray, Build Dam, Ritual bath, Acupuncture, Cut hair, Clean Floor, Brew Wine, Collect Money, Take Animal, Planting, Herding, Fix Floor, Break Ground, Burial, Fill Hole		**Bad** Pay Tribute, Marriage, Opening, Fix Bed	

13 Saturday 乙酉 Wood Rooster	**Clash** Rabbit	**Influence**	**12 Rulers** Establish	**Flying star** 9
	Good Pray, Ritual bath, Clean Floor		**Bad** Visiting relatives, Gathering, New Construction, Buy House, Demolish	

September

14 **Sunday** 丙戌 **Fire Dog**	**Clash** Dragon	**Influence**	**12 Rulers** Removal	**Flying star** 8
	Good Clean house, Pray, Ritual bath, Receive award, Cut hair, Travel, Cut Nail, New Job, Clean Floor, Politics, Planting, Public relation			**Bad** Marriage, Opening, Burial, Sign contract

15 **Monday** 丁亥 **Fire Pig**	**Clash** Snake	**Influence** ❶	**12 Rulers** Fulfill	**Flying star** 7
	Good Pray, Ritual bath, Sewing, Pay Tribute, Acupuncture, Move House, Opening, Policy review, Sign contract, Travel, Fix Floor, Trading, Collect Money, Fill Hole			**Bad** New Job, Marriage, Boating, Burial

16 **Tuesday** 戊子 **Earth Rat**	**Clash** Horse	**Influence**	**12 Rulers** Balance	**Flying star** 6
	Good Pray, Ritual bath, Decoration, Paint Wall, Repair Road			**Bad** Pay Tribute, Marriage, Travel, Opening

17 **Wednesday** 己丑 **Earth Ox**	**Clash** Goat	**Influence**	**12 Rulers** Stability	**Flying star** 5
	Good Engagement, Visiting relatives, Gathering, Sewing, Marriage, Brew Wine, Repair House, Sign contract, New Construction, Erect pole, Trading, Collect Money, Herding, Fix warehouse, Acupuncture, Take Animal			**Bad** Mitzvah, Buy House, Planting

September

18 Thursday 庚寅 Metal Tiger	Clash Monkey	Influence ❸ ❹		12 Rulers Control	Flying star 4
	Good Ritual bath, Pest Control			**Bad** Opening, Move House, Return Home Land, Sign contract	

19 Friday 辛卯 Metal Rabbit	Clash Rooster	Influence ❷ ❸ ❹		12 Rulers Clash	Flying star 3
	Good Demolish, Break Floor			**Bad** Major Moves	

20 Saturday 壬辰 Water Dragon	Clash Dog	Influence ❸ ❹		12 Rulers Danger	Flying star 2
	Good Pray			**Bad** Fix Sewage, Recuperate, Receive award	

21 Sunday 癸巳 Water Snake	Clash Pig	Influence		12 Rulers Accomplish	Flying star 1
	Good Engagement, Pray, Pay Tribute, Marriage, Visiting relatives, Repair House, Gathering, New Construction, New school, Opening, New Job, Sign contract, Move House, Adoption			**Bad** Travel, Burial, Break Ground	

September

22 **Monday** 甲午 **Wood Horse**	Clash Rat	Influence ❺	12 Rulers Harvest	Flying star 9
	Good Pray, Pest Control			**Bad** Trading, Move House, Burial, Marriage

23 **Tuesday** 乙未 **Wood Goat**	Clash Ox	Influence ❹	12 Rulers Opening	Flying star 8
	Good Engagement, Pray, Pay Tribute, Marriage, Opening, Pray for Progeny, Visiting relatives, Cast Beam, Gathering, Herding, New school, Take Animal, Travel, Wedding gift, New Job, Clean house, Propose marriage			**Bad** Demolish, Repair House, Break Floor, New Construction

24 **Wednesday** 丙申 **Fire Monkey**	Clash Tiger	Influence ❷ ❹	12 Rulers Closing	Flying star 7
	Good Brew Wine, Pray, Collect Money, Ritual bath, Clean Floor, Cut hair, Herding, Cut Nail, Sewing, Take Animal, Acupuncture, Burial			**Bad** Visiting relatives, Gathering, Travel, Fix Bed, Move House

25 **Thursday** 丁酉 **Fire Rooster**	Clash Rabbit	Influence ❹	12 Rulers Establish	Flying star 6
	Good Pray			**Bad** Fix Sewage, Recuperate, Receive Award

September

26 Friday 戊戌 Earth Dog	Clash	Influence	12 Rulers	Flying star
	Dragon		Removal	5
	Good			**Bad**
	Clean house, Pray, Receive award, Ritual bath, Cut hair, Receive award, Travel, Cut Nail, New Job, Clean Floor, New Job, Planting, Politics, Public relation			Break Ground, Buy House, Burial

27 Saturday 己亥 Earth Pig	Clash	Influence	12 Rulers	Flying star
	Snake	❶	Fulfill	4
	Good			**Bad**
	Sewing, Pray, Acupuncture, Pay Tribute, Opening, Policy review, Sign contract, Visiting relatives, Gathering, Trading, Travel, Collect Money, Fix Floor, Ritual bath, Adoption, Fill Hole			Receive award, New Job,

28 Sunday 庚子 Metal Rat	Clash	Influence	12 Rulers	Flying star
	Horse		Balance	3
	Good			**Bad**
	Pray, Ritual bath, Decoration, Paint Wall, Repair Road			Hunting, Travel, Fishing, Move House

29 Monday 辛丑 Metal Ox	Clash	Influence	12 Rulers	Flying star
	Goat		Stability	2
	Good			**Bad**
	Visiting relatives, Gathering, Sewing, Fix warehouse, Delivery, Acupuncture, Collect Money			Mitzvah, Wedding gift, Propose marriage, Marriage

175

September

30 Tuesday 壬寅 Water Tiger	Clash Monkey	Influence ❸ ❹		12 Rulers Control	Flying star 1
	Good			Bad	
	Ritual bath, Pest Control			Repair House, Break Ground, New Construction, Burial	

October

1 Wednesday 癸卯 Water Rabbit	Clash Rooster	Influence ❷ ❸ ❹	12 Rulers Clash	Flying star 9
	Good		Bad	
	Demolish, Break Floor		Rashly Action	

2 Thursday 甲辰 Wood Dragon	Clash Dog	Influence ❸ ❹ ❼	12 Rulers Danger	Flying star 8
	Good		Bad	
	Planting, Policy review, Planning, Take Animal, Herding, Engagement, Donation, Marriage, Appeal, Rewarding, Sign contract, Banquet, Burial, Fix Altar, Collect Money		Repair House, Travel, New Construction, New Job	

3 Friday 乙巳 Wood Snake	Clash Pig	Influence ❼	12 Rulers Accomplish	Flying star 7
	Good		Bad	
	Engagement, Pray, Pay Tribute, Marriage, Repair House, Pray for Progeny, Visiting relatives, New Construction, Gathering, Opening, New school, Sign contract, New Job, Acupuncture, Move House, Brew Wine, Clean house		Hunting, Travel, Planting, Fishing	

October

4 Saturday 丙午 Fire Horse	Clash: Rat	Influence:	12 Rulers: Harvest	Flying star: 6
	Good Pray, Pest Control			Bad Marriage, Boating, Engagement

5 Sunday 丁未 Fire Goat	Clash: Ox	Influence:	12 Rulers: Opening	Flying star: 5
	Good Pray, New Job, Pay Tribute, New Job, Politics, Public relation, Receive award, Clean house, Visiting relatives, Gathering, Sewing, New school, Erect pole, Travel, Cast Beam, Move House			Bad Trading, Opening, Payment, Sign contract

6 Monday 戊申 Earth Monkey	Clash: Tiger	Influence:	12 Rulers: Closing	Flying star: 4
	Good Acupuncture Pray, Brew Wine, Ritual bath, Cut hair, Sign contract, Trading, Cut Nail, Sewing, Collect Money, Fix Floor, Build Dam, Planting, Fix warehouse, Burial, Take Animal			Bad Pay Tribute, Fix Bed, Eye care, Pray for Progeny

7 Tuesday 己酉 Earth Rooster	Clash: Rabbit	Influence:	12 Rulers: Establish	Flying star: 3
	Good Pray			Bad Repair House, New Construction

October

8 Wednesday 庚戌 **Metal Dog**	**Clash** Dragon	**Influence**	**12 Rulers** Establish	**Flying star** 2
	Good Pray, Visiting relatives, Gathering, Travel, New Job, Move House, Sewing, Herding, Take Animal			**Bad** Cut hair, New Construction, Buy House, Burial

9 Thursday 辛亥 **Metal Pig**	**Clash** Snake	**Influence** ❶ ❹	**12 Rulers** Removal	**Flying star** 1
	Good Clean house, Pray, Pay Tribute, Ritual bath, Cut hair, Pray for Progeny, Cut Nail, Receive award, Sewing, Visiting relatives, Gathering, Cast Beam, Travel, Clean Floor, New Job, Take Animal, Move House			**Bad** Marriage, New Construction, Burial, Opening

10 Friday 壬子 **Water Rat**	**Clash** Horse	**Influence** ❹	**12 Rulers** Fulfill	**Flying star** 9
	Good Pray, Ritual bath			**Bad** Marriage, Move House, Sign contract, Burial

11 Saturday 癸丑 **Water Ox**	**Clash** Goat	**Influence** ❹	**12 Rulers** Balance	**Flying star** 8
	Good Be Careful			**Bad** Be Conservative

October

12 **Sunday** 甲寅 **Wood Tiger**	Clash Monkey	Influence ❸	12 Rulers Stability	Flying star 7
	Good Donation, Appeal, Rewarding, Break Ground			Bad Pray, Marriage, Burial, Opening

13 **Monday** 乙卯 **Wood Rabbit**	Clash Rooster	Influence ❸	12 Rulers Control	Flying star 6
	Good Pray, Pest Control, Hunting			Bad Move House, Fix Bed, New Construction, Marriage

14 **Tuesday** 丙辰 **Fire Dragon**	Clash Dog	Influence ❷ ❸	12 Rulers Clash	Flying star 5
	Good Pray, Clean house, Ritual bath, Demolish, Break Floor			Bad Pay Tribute, Cut hair, Sign contract, Burial

15 **Wednesday** 丁巳 **Fire Snake**	Clash Pig	Influence	12 Rulers Danger	Flying star 4
	Good Pray, Fix Bed, Hunting			Bad Pray, Fix Bed, Hunting

October

16 **Thursday** 戊午 **Earth Horse**	**Clash** Rat	**Influence**	**12 Rulers** Accomplish	**Flying star** 3
	Good Visiting relatives, Wedding gift, Gathering, Marriage, New school, Build Dam, Travel, Repair House, New Job, New Construction, Move House, Erect pole, Brew Wine, Take Animal, Opening, Acupuncture, Sign contract		**Bad** New Construction, Burial	

17 **Friday** 己未 **Earth Goat**	**Clash** Ox	**Influence**	**12 Rulers** Harvest	**Flying star** 2
	Good Pest Control, Hunting		**Bad** Be Conservative	

18 **Saturday** 庚申 **Metal Monkey**	**Clash** Tiger	**Influence**	**12 Rulers** Opening	**Flying star** 1
	Good Cut hair, Pray, Pay Tribute, Cut Nail, Sewing, Pray for Progeny, Repair House, New school, New Construction, New Job, Fix Sewage, Move House, Clean house, Dig Well, Opening, Ritual bath		**Bad** Visiting relatives, Sign contract, Gathering, Marriage, Fix Bed	

19 **Sunday** 辛酉 **Metal Rooster**	**Clash** Rabbit	**Influence**	**12 Rulers** Closing	**Flying star** 9
	Good Pray, Ritual bath, Clean Floor, Cut Nail, Cut hair, Fix Floor, Fill Hole		**Bad** Acupuncture, Visiting relatives, Gathering, Brew Wine, Eye care	

October

20 **Monday** 壬戌 **Water Dog**	**Clash** Dragon	**Influence**	**12 Rulers** Establish	**Flying star** 8
	Good Engagement, Pray, Pay Tribute, Wedding gift, Receive award, Propose marriage, Erect pole, Receive award, Cast Beam, Travel, Take Animal, New Job, Visiting relatives, Policy review, Gathering			**Bad** Buy House, Repair House, New Construction

21 **Tuesday** 癸亥 **Water Pig**	**Clash** Snake	**Influence** ❶ ❹	**12 Rulers** Removal	**Flying star** 7
	Good Pray, Ritual bath, Clean Floor			**Bad** Fix Sewage, Marriage, Dig Well, Burial

22 **Wednesday** 甲子 **Wood Rat**	**Clash** Horse	**Influence** ❹	**12 Rulers** Fulfill	**Flying star** 6
	Good Pray, Ritual bath			**Bad** Repair House, Build Dam, New Construction, Cast Beam

23 **Thursday** 乙丑 **Wood Ox**	**Clash** Goat	**Influence** ❹	**12 Rulers** Balance	**Flying star** 5
	Good Be Careful			**Bad** Rashly Action

October

24 **Friday** 丙寅 **Fire Tiger**	Clash Monkey	Influence ③	12 Rulers Stability	Flying star 4
	Good Donation, Appeal, Planting			Bad New Job, Travel, New Job, Move House

25 **Saturday** 丁卯 **Fire Rabbit**	Clash Rooster	Influence ③	12 Rulers Control	Flying star 3
	Good Engagement, Pray, Pay Tribute, Marriage, Pest Control, Visiting relatives, Hunting, Gathering, Acupuncture, Take Animal, Brew Wine, Break Ground, Adoption, Burial			Bad Cut hair, Opening, Sign contract, Fix warehouse

26 **Sunday** 戊辰 **Earth Dragon**	Clash Dog	Influence ② ③	12 Rulers Clash	Flying star 2
	Good Pray, Ritual bath, Demolish, Break Floor			Bad Repair House, Marriage, Buy House, Sign contract,

27 **Monday** 己巳 **Earth Snake**	Clash Pig	Influence	12 Rulers Danger	Flying star 1
	Good Pray, Fix Bed, Hunting			Bad Acupuncture, Break Ground, Burial, Recuperate

October

28 Tuesday 庚午 Metal Horse	Clash Rat	Influence	12 Rulers Accomplish	Flying star 9
	Good Engagement, Pray, Pay Tribute, Marriage, New Construction, Pray for Progeny, Visiting relatives, Opening, Gathering, Sign contract, New school, Take Animal, Travel, Break Ground, New Job, Burial, Move House			**Bad** Acupuncture

29 Wednesday 辛未 Metal Goat	Clash Ox	Influence	12 Rulers Harvest	Flying star 8
	Good Pray, Pest Control			**Bad** Repair Road, Demolish, Break Floor

30 Thursday 壬申 Water Monkey	Clash Tiger	Influence	12 Rulers Opening	Flying star 7
	Good Pray, Repair House, Pay Tribute, New Construction, Buy House, New school, Opening, Travel, Collect Money, New Job, Move House, Cut hair, Clean Floor, Sewing			**Bad** Boating, Visiting relatives, Gathering, Marriage, Sign contract

31 Friday 癸酉 Water Rooster	Clash Rabbit	Influence	12 Rulers Closing	Flying star 6
	Good Donation, Rewarding, Banquet, Travel, Sewing			**Bad** Mitzvah, Break Ground, Burial, Fix Bed

November

1 **Saturday** 甲戌 **Wood Dog**	**Clash** Dragon	**Influence**	**12 Rulers** Establish	**Flying star** 5
	Good Pray		**Bad** Repair House, New Construction,	

2 **Sunday** 乙亥 **Wood Pig**	**Clash** Snake	**Influence** ❶ ❹	**12 Rulers** Removal	**Flying star** 4
	Good Pray, Clean Floor		**Bad** Fix Floor, Decoration, Paint Wall, Fill Hole	

3 **Monday** 丙子 **Fire Rat**	**Clash** Horse	**Influence** ❹	**12 Rulers** Fulfill	**Flying star** 3
	Good Engagement, Pray, Pay Tribute, Marriage, Opening, Pray for Progeny, Visiting relatives, Sign contract, Gathering, Fix Floor, Travel, Fill Hole, New Job, Break Ground, New Job, Burial, Policy review			**Bad** Boating, Move House, Return Home Land, Fishing

4 **Tuesday** 丁丑 **Fire Ox**	**Clash** Goat	**Influence** ❹	**12 Rulers** Balance	**Flying star** 2
	Good Be Careful		**Bad** Be Conservative	

November

5 Wednesday 戊寅 **Earth Tiger**	**Clash** Monkey	**Influence** ❸		**12 Rulers** Stability	**Flying star** 1
	Good Recuperate, Appeal			**Bad** Be Conservative	

6 Thursday 己卯 **Earth Rabbit**	**Clash** Rooster	**Influence** ❸ ❻	**12 Rulers** Control	**Flying star** 9
	Good Engagement, Pray, Pay Tribute, Marriage, Pest Control, Acupuncture, Hunting, Brew Wine, Take Animal, Burial, Visiting relatives, Adoption, Gathering		**Bad** Payment, Opening, Dig Well, Sign contract	

7 Friday 庚辰 **Metal Dragon**	**Clash** Dog	**Influence** ❷ * ❸	**12 Rulers** Clash	**Flying star** 8
	Good Pray, Clean house,		**Bad** Engagement, Fix Bed, Buy House, Marriage,	

8 Saturday 辛巳 **Metal Snake**	**Clash** Pig	**Influence** ❷	**12 Rulers** Clash	**Flying star** 7
	Good Visit Doctor, Recuperate, Demolish, Break Floor		**Bad** Move House, Marriage, Burial, Repair House	

* 7 NOV - Bomb 4: Valid **before** 12:06

November

9 **Sunday** 壬午 **Water Horse**	**Clash** Rat	**Influence**	**12 Rulers** Danger	**Flying star** 6
	Good Pray, Visiting relatives, Gathering, Sewing, Logging, Hunting		**Bad** Pay Tribute, Travel, Burial, Marriage	

10 **Monday** 癸未 **Water Goat**	**Clash** Ox	**Influence**	**12 Rulers** Accomplish	**Flying star** 5
	Good Pray, Build Dam, Pay Tribute, Repair House, Visiting relatives, New Construction, Gathering, Erect pole, New school, Fix warehouse, Wedding gift, Sewing, Opening, Brew Wine, Sign contract, Take Animal, Trading		**Bad** Travel, Marriage, Move House, New Job	

11 **Tuesday** 甲申 **Wood Monkey**	**Clash** Tiger	**Influence** ❹	**12 Rulers** Harvest	**Flying star** 4
	Good Pray, Marriage, Pay Tribute, Wedding gift, Cut hair, Pray for Progeny, Visiting relatives, Cut Nail, Gathering, Repair House, Travel, New Construction, New Job, Logging, Break Ground, Burial, Take Animal		**Bad** Fix Bed, Delivery, Hunting, Fishing	

12 **Wednesday** 乙酉 **Wood Rooster**	**Clash** Rabbit	**Influence** ❹	**12 Rulers** Opening	**Flying star** 3
	Good Pray, Marriage, Pay Tribute, Wedding gift, Cut hair, Pray for Progeny, Cut Nail, New school, Sewing, Travel, Opening, Move House, Buy House, New Construction.		**Bad** Visiting relatives, Logging, Gathering, Planting, Fishing	

November

13 Thursday
丙戌
Fire Dog

Clash	Influence	12 Rulers	Flying star
Dragon	❹	Closing	2

Good	Bad
Be Careful	Rashly Action

14 Friday
丁亥
Fire Pig

Clash	Influence	12 Rulers	Flying star
Snake	❶	Establish	1

Good	Bad
Pray, Ritual bath	Think Thrice, Except above

15 Saturday
戊子
Earth Rat

Clash	Influence	12 Rulers	Flying star
Horse		Removal	9

Good	Bad
Ritual bath, Clean Floor	Banquet

16 Sunday
己丑
Earth Ox

Clash	Influence	12 Rulers	Flying star
Goat		Fulfill	8

Good	Bad
Pray	Travel, Marriage, Move House, Fishing

November

17 Monday 庚寅 Metal Tiger	Clash Monkey	Influence ③	12 Rulers Balance	Flying star 7
	Good			Bad
	Engagement, Visiting relatives, Gathering, Marriage, Travel, Repair House, New Job, New Construction, Move House, Sewing, Cast Beam, Brew Wine, Opening, Herding, Sign contract, Burial, Take Animal			Clean house, Pray, Acupuncture, Pay Tribute

18 Tuesday 辛卯 Metal Rabbit	Clash Rooster	Influence ③	12 Rulers Stability	Flying star 6
	Good			Bad
	Engagement, Receive award, Visiting relatives, Marriage, Gathering, Mitzvah, Repair House, Opening, Travel, Sign contract, New Job, Trading, Move House, Acupuncture, Break Ground, Burial, Take Animal			Buy House, Clean house, Brew Wine, Dig Well

19 Wednesday 壬辰 Water Dragon	Clash Dog	Influence ③	12 Rulers Control	Flying star 5
	Good			Bad
	Policy review, Ritual bath, Cut hair, Cut Nail, Sewing, Pest Control, Hunting			New Job, Travel, New Job, Move House

20 Thursday 癸巳 Water Snake	Clash Pig	Influence ②	12 Rulers Clash	Flying star 4
	Good			Bad
	Demolish, Break Floor, Visit Doctor, Recuperate			Engagement, Repair House, New Construction, Marriage

November

21 **Friday** 甲午 **Wood Horse**	**Clash** Rat	**Influence**	**12 Rulers** Danger	**Flying star** 3
	Good Engagement, Pray, Pay Tribute, Marriage, Repair House, Policy review, Visiting relatives, New Construction, Gathering, Cast Beam, Travel, Fix warehouse, New Job, Logging, Move House, Burial, Fix Bed			**Bad** Hunting, Fishing, Payment

22 **Saturday** 乙未 **Wood Goat**	**Clash** Ox	**Influence**	**12 Rulers** Accomplish	**Flying star** 2
	Good Engagement, Pray, Pay Tribute, Repair House, New Construction, Pray for Progeny, Visiting relatives, Cast Beam, Gathering, Fix warehouse, New school, Clean house, Opening, Acupuncture, Sign contract, Brew Wine, Burial			**Bad** Marriage, Travel, Move House, New Job

23 **Sunday** 丙申 **Fire Monkey**	**Clash** Tiger	**Influence** ❹	**12 Rulers** Harvest	**Flying star** 1
	Good Ritual bath, Pest Control, Clean Floor, Logging, Hunting			**Bad** Buy House, Opening, Trading, Sign contract

24 **Monday** 丁酉 **Fire Rooster**	**Clash** Rabbit	**Influence** ❹	**12 Rulers** Opening	**Flying star** 9
	Good Pray, Ritual bath, New school, Clean Floor			**Bad** Cut hair, Visiting relatives, Gathering, Acupuncture, Mitzvah

November

25 **Tuesday** 戊戌 **Earth Dog**	**Clash** Dragon	**Influence** ❹	**12 Rulers** Closing	**Flying star** 8
	Good Build Dam, Fix Floor, Fill Hole			**Bad** Think Thrice, Except above

26 **Wednesday** 己亥 **Earth Pig**	**Clash** Snake	**Influence** ❶	**12 Rulers** Establish	**Flying star** 7
	Good Pray, Ritual bath			**Bad** Repair House,| New Construction

27 **Thursday** 庚子 **Metal Rat**	**Clash** Horse	**Influence**	**12 Rulers** Removal	**Flying star** 6
	Good Engagement, Pray, Visiting relatives, Marriage, Gathering, Repair House, Travel, New Construction, New Job, Cut hair, Move House, Break Ground, Cut Nail, Clean house, Clean Floor, Burial			**Bad** Acupuncture, Hunting, Fishing

28 **Friday** 辛丑 **Metal Ox**	**Clash** Goat	**Influence**	**12 Rulers** Fulfill	**Flying star** 5
	Good Pray			**Bad** Engagement, Wedding gift, Propose marriage, Marriage

November

29 Saturday 壬寅 Water Tiger	Clash Monkey	Influence ❸		12 Rulers Balance	Flying star 4
	Good			Bad	
	Engagement, Marriage, Receive award, Visiting relatives, Repair House, Gathering, Paint Wall, Travel, Opening, New Job, Sign contract, Move House, Adoption, Shipments, Payment			Pray, Pray for Progeny, Pay Tribute, Fix Sewage,	

30 Sunday 癸卯 Water Rabbit	Clash Rooster	Influence ❸		12 Rulers Stability	Flying star 3
	Good			Bad	
	Engagement, Receive award, Visiting relatives, Marriage, Gathering, Mitzvah, Opening, Sign contract, Travel, Trading, New Job, Take Animal, Move House, Break Ground, Repair House, Burial, New Construction			Buy House, Clean house, Planting, Dig Well	

December

1 Monday 甲辰 Wood Dragon	Clash Dog	Influence ❸ ❼	12 Rulers Control	Flying star 2
	Good		Bad	
	Engagement, Pray, Pay Tribute, Marriage, Cut hair, Pray for Progeny, Visiting relatives, Cut Nail, Gathering, Pest Control, New Job, Herding, Move House, Clean house, Take Animal, Burial, Ritual bath		Repair House, Travel, Dig Well, Build Dam	

2 Tuesday 乙巳 Wood Snake	Clash Pig	Influence ❷ ❼	12 Rulers Clash	Flying star 1
	Good		Bad	
	Pray, Demolish, Break Floor, Clean house, Recuperate		Opening, Marriage, Buy House, Repair House	

December

3 **Wednesday** 丙午 **Fire Horse**	**Clash** Rat	**Influence**	**12 Rulers** Danger	**Flying star** 9
	Good Pray, Logging, Hunting		**Bad** Buy House, Fix Bed, Cast Beam, Fix warehouse	

4 **Thursday** 丁未 **Fire Goat**	**Clash** Ox	**Influence**	**12 Rulers** Accomplish	**Flying star** 8
	Good Pray, Repair House, Pay Tribute, New Construction, Erect pole, Visiting relatives, Gathering, Cast Beam, New school, Acupuncture, Sewing, Brew Wine, Build Dam, Opening, Fix warehouse, Sign contract, Take Animal		**Bad** Boating, Travel, Cut hair, Marriage	

5 **Friday** 戊申 **Earth Monkey**	**Clash** Tiger	**Influence** ❹	**12 Rulers** Harvest	**Flying star** 7
	Good Ritual bath, Logging, Clean Floor, Pest Control, Hunting		**Bad** Demolish, Repair Road, Break Floor	

6 **Saturday** 己酉 **Earth Rooster**	**Clash** Rabbit	**Influence** ❹	**12 Rulers** Opening	**Flying star** 6
	Good Engagement, Pray, Pay Tribute, Marriage, Repair House, Pray for Progeny, New Construction, New school, Opening, Travel, Buy House, Move House, Clean house, Fix Sewage, Cut hair, Dig Well		**Bad** Hunting, Visiting relatives, Gathering, Logging, Fishing	

December

7 **Sunday** 庚戌 **Metal Dog**	Clash	Influence	12 Rulers	Flying star
	Dragon	❹ *	Opening	5
	Good			**Bad**
	Visiting relatives, Pray, Gathering, Pay Tribute, New school, Clean house, Pray for Progeny, Sewing, Repair House, Planting, New Construction, Herding, Erect pole, Buy House, Fix Sewage, Dig Well			Opening, Marriage, Travel, Move House

8 **Monday** 辛亥 **Metal Pig**	Clash	Influence	12 Rulers	Flying star
	Snake	❶	Closing	4
	Good			**Bad**
	Ritual bath, Sewing, Build Dam, Fix Floor, Fill Hole			Marriage, Travel, Burial, Opening

9 **Tuesday** 壬子 **Water Rat**	Clash	Influence	12 Rulers	Flying star
	Horse		Establish	3
	Good			**Bad**
	Be Careful			Big Changes

10 **Wednesday** 癸丑	Clash	Influence	12 Rulers	Flying star
	Goat		Removal	2
	Good			**Bad**
	Pray, Marriage, Pay Tribute, Wedding gift, Cut hair, Pray for Progeny, Repair House, Travel, Visiting relatives, New Construction, Gathering, Cut Nail, New Job, Brew Wine, Opening, Take Animal, Sign contract			Mitzvah, Fishing, Boating, Cross River

* 7 DEC- Bomb 4: Valid **before** 05:06

193

December

11 Thursday 甲寅 Wood Tiger	Clash Monkey	Influence ❸	12 Rulers Fulfill	Flying star 1
	Good		Bad	
	Repair House, Receive award, Visiting relatives, New Construction, Gathering, Erect pole, Travel, Cast Beam, New Job, Clean house, Sewing, Fix Floor, Opening, Planting, Sign contract, Break Ground		Pray, Marriage, Boating, Move House	

12 Friday 乙卯 Wood Rabbit	Clash Rooster	Influence ❸	12 Rulers Balance	Flying star 9
	Good		Bad	
	Be Careful		Be Conservative	

13 Saturday 丙辰 Fire Dragon	Clash Dog	Influence ❸	12 Rulers Stability	Flying star 8
	Good		Bad	
	Pray, Marriage, Pay Tribute, Wedding gift, Sewing, Receive award, Visiting relatives, Repair House, Gathering, New Construction, New Job, Cast Beam, Sign contract, Fix warehouse, Trading,		Clean house, Buy House, Planting, Recuperate	

14 Sunday 丁巳 Fire Snake	Clash Pig	Influence ❹	12 Rulers Control	Flying star 7
	Good		Bad	
	Pray, Pest Control		Travel, Marriage, Burial, Opening	

December

15 Monday 戊午 Earth Horse	Clash Rat	Influence ❷ ❹	12 Rulers Clash	Flying star 6
	Good Be Careful			Bad Be Conservative

16 Tuesday 己未 Earth Goat	Clash Ox	Influence ❹	12 Rulers Danger	Flying star 5
	Good Logging, Hunting			Bad Major Changes

17 Wednesday 庚申 Metal Monkey	Clash Tiger	Influence	12 Rulers Accomplish	Flying star 4
	Good Cast Beam, Receive award, Brew Wine, Visiting relatives, Gathering, Opening, New school, Sign contract, Travel, Logging, New Job, Clean Floor, Move House, Clean house, Take Animal, Cut hair, Burial			Bad Buy House, Demolish, Paint Wall, New Construction

18 Thursday 辛酉 Metal Rooster	Clash Rabbit	Influence	12 Rulers Harvest	Flying star 3
	Good Ritual bath, Cut hair, Cut Nail, Clean Floor, Pest Control, Hunting			Bad Mitzvah, Pay Tribute, Burial, Pray for Progeny

December

19 **Friday** 壬戌 **Water Dog**	**Clash** Dragon	**Influence**	**12 Rulers** Opening	**Flying star** 2
	Good Engagement, Pray, Pay Tribute, Wedding gift, Clean house, Pray for Progeny, Planting, Visiting relatives, Gathering, Opening, New school, Buy House, Repair House, Herding, New Construction			**Bad** Marriage, Travel, Logging, Move House

20 **Saturday** 癸亥 **Water Pig**	**Clash** Snake	**Influence** ❶ ❺	**12 Rulers** Closing	**Flying star** 1
	Good Fast-bat			**Bad** Pay Tribute, Fix Bed, Buy House, Pray for Progeny

21 **Sunday** 甲子 **Wood Rat**	**Clash** Horse	**Influence**	**12 Rulers** Establish	**Flying star** 1
	Good Pray, Ritual bath			**Bad** Think Thrice, Except above

22 **Monday** 乙丑 **Wood Ox**	**Clash** Goat	**Influence**	**12 Rulers** Removal	**Flying star** 2
	Good Engagement, Pray, Pay Tribute, Marriage, Repair House, Pray for Progeny, Visiting relatives, New Construction, Gathering, Sign contract, Travel, Cut Nail, New Job, Take Animal, Move House, Cut hair, Burial			**Bad** Mitzvah, Planting

December

23 Tuesday
丙寅
Fire Tiger

Clash	Influence	12 Rulers	Flying star
Monkey	❸	Fulfill	3

Good: Repair House, Receive Award, New Construction, Opening, Policy review, Visiting relatives, Cast Beam, Gathering, Travel, Clean house, Sign contract, Fix Floor, Acupuncture, Adoption, Break Ground

Bad: New Job, Marriage, Return Home Land, Move House

24 Wednesday
丁卯
Fire Rabbit

Clash	Influence	12 Rulers	Flying star
Rooster	❸	Balance	4

Good: Pray, Repair Road

Bad: Rashly Action

25 Thursday
戊辰
Earth Dragon

Clash	Influence	12 Rulers	Flying star
Dog	❸	Stability	5

Good: Engagement, Pray, Pay Tribute, Marriage, Repair House, Visiting relatives, New Construction, Gathering, Mitzvah, Sign contract, Brew Wine, New Job, Adoption

Bad: Buy House, Clean house, Planting, Recuperate

26 Friday
己巳
Earth Snake

Clash	Influence	12 Rulers	Flying star
Pig	❹	Control	6

Good: Pray, Pest Control, Hunting

Bad: Marriage, Travel, Opening, Move House

December

27 Saturday 庚午 Metal Horse	Clash Rat	Influence ❷ ❹		12 Rulers Clash	Flying star 7
	Good Demolish, Break Floor			Bad Think Thrice	

28 Sunday 辛未 Metal Goat	Clash Ox	Influence ❹		12 Rulers Danger	Flying star 8
	Good Logging, Hunting			Bad Major Moves	

29 Monday 壬申 Water Monkey	Clash Tiger	Influence		12 Rulers Accomplish	Flying star 9
	Good Engagement, Pray, Pay Tribute, Marriage, Opening, Pray for Progeny, Visiting relatives, Sign contract, Gathering, Cut hair, New school, Clean house, Travel, Acupuncture, New Job, Burial, Move House			Bad Fix Sewage, Fix Bed, Fix Floor, Repair House	

30 Tuesday 癸酉 Water Rooster	Clash Rabbit	Influence		12 Rulers Harvest	Flying star 1
	Good Ritual bath, Cut hair, Cut Nail, Clean Floor, Pest Control, Hunting			Bad Buy House, Opening, Payment, Sign contract	

December

31 Wednesday 甲戌 **Wood Dog**	**Clash** Dragon	**Influence**		**12 Rulers** Opening	**Flying star** 2
	Good Engagement, Pray, Pay Tribute, Repair House, New Construction, Pray for Progeny, Buy House, Visiting relatives, Gathering, Dig Well, New school, Clean house, Fix Sewage, Sewing, Cast Beam, Herding, Planting			**Bad** Marriage, Travel, Opening, Move House	

199

JANUARY — HOURS

Day	23:00-01:00	01:00-03:00	03:00-05:00	05:00-07:00	07:00-09:00	09:00-11:00	11:00-13:00	13:00-15:00	15:00-17:00	17:00-19:00	19:00-21:00	21:00-23:00
1	●	○	○	◎	●	●	◎	○	○	◎	●	●
2	●	●	◎	◎	●	◎	○	○	◎	●	○	●
3	◎	◎	●	○	◎	◎	○	◎	●	●	○	●
4	○	●	◎	◎	◎	○	◎	●	○	●	●	●
5	●	○	◎	○	○	◎	●	○	○	○	○	◎
6	○	◎	○	○	◎	●	○	○	◎	●	◎	◎
7	◎	◎	○	○	●	●	○	●	○	◎	○	○
8	○	○	○	●	●	◎	○	●	○	◎	○	◎
9	○	◎	●	○	◎	○	●	◎	○	●	○	○
10	◎	●	◎	◎	●	○	◎	◎	○	●	○	○
11	●	○	◎	●	○	◎	◎	○	○	○	●	◎
12	●	◎	○	●	○	◎	◎	○	●	○	◎	◎
13	○	○	●	◎	○	○	◎	◎	●	○	●	○
14	●	●	◎	◎	◎	◎	○	●	○	●	◎	○
15	◎	◎	◎	●	◎	◎	●	◎	●	○	◎	●
16	◎	○	◎	○	○	●	●	●	◎	○	●	◎
17	◎	●	○	●	○	○	●	●	◎	◎	◎	◎
18	●	◎	○	●	◎	○	◎	○	●	◎	◎	◎
19	○	◎	●	◎	○	○	○	○	◎	◎	●	●
20	◎	●	◎	◎	●	◎	●	○	◎	●	○	○
21	○	◎	○	●	◎	○	◎	○	○	●	○	○
22	○	●	◎	◎	●	◎	○	○	○	○	○	○
23	●	○	○	○	◎	◎	○	○	●	◎	●	◎
24	○	○	●	◎	◎	◎	○	●	○	●	◎	○
25	○	○	◎	◎	●	●	●	◎	○	◎	●	●
26	○	○	◎	◎	●	●	○	○	◎	●	◎	◎
27	◎	◎	●	●	●	○	○	◎	○	○	◎	○
28	◎	●	○	●	○	●	◎	◎	●	◎	●	◎
29	●	○	●	◎	○	○	●	○	◎	○	○	○
30	○	●	◎	●	○	●	◎	○	●	◎	●	●
31	○	◎	○	○	●	●	◎	○	◎	◎	●	●

GOOD ◎   FAIR ○   BAD ●

FEBRUARY — HOURS

	23:00–01:00	01:00–03:00	03:00–05:00	05:00–07:00	07:00–09:00	09:00–11:00	11:00–13:00	13:00–15:00	15:00–17:00	17:00–19:00	19:00–21:00	21:00–23:00
1	○	○	◎	◎	●	◎	○	●	◎	●	○	◎
2	◎	◎	○	○	◎	○	○	◎	●	●	◎	○
3	○	●	◎	◎	○	○	◎	●	●	○	○	●
4	●	○	◎	●	○	◎	●	○	○	◎	●	◎
5	○	◎	●	○	◎	●	○	○	◎	●	◎	◎
6	◎	○	◎	○	●	○	○	◎	◎	○	○	◎
7	●	●	○	●	●	◎	◎	○	◎	◎	◎	◎
8	○	◎	●	○	◎	◎	●	◎	◎	●	○	●
9	◎	●	◎	○	○	●	◎	◎	○	○	●	●
10	●	○	○	○	○	○	◎	○	◎	○	●	◎
11	●	◎	○	●	○	◎	◎	◎	○	●	●	○
12	◎	◎	●	○	●	◎	○	●	◎	◎	●	●
13	○	○	○	◎	◎	◎	●	●	◎	●	○	○
14	○	◎	◎	●	◎	○	●	◎	●	○	◎	○
15	○	○	◎	◎	●	●	○	○	◎	○	○	○
16	◎	●	◎	●	●	○	●	●	◎	◎	○	○
17	●	○	●	●	◎	○	◎	◎	○	◎	◎	◎
18	●	○	●	◎	○	○	○	◎	◎	◎	●	●
19	○	●	◎	◎	●	◎	○	◎	◎	●	◎	○
20	○	◎	●	●	◎	◎	◎	○	○	●	○	●
21	○	●	◎	○	○	◎	◎	◎	○	○	●	○
22	●	○	○	○	◎	◎	○	○	○	○	○	◎
23	●	○	○	◎	◎	○	◎	○	●	●	◎	○
24	◎	◎	◎	○	●	●	●	○	○	○	●	●
25	○	○	◎	◎	●	●	◎	●	◎	●	○	●
26	◎	◎	○	●	●	○	●	◎	○	○	○	○
27	○	●	○	●	●	○	◎	◎	●	◎	○	○
28	●	○	○	○	◎	◎	●	○	◎	◎	●	○
29												
30												
31												

GOOD ◎   FAIR ○   BAD ●

MARCH HOURS

Day	23:00–01:00	01:00–03:00	03:00–05:00	05:00–07:00	07:00–09:00	09:00–11:00	11:00–13:00	13:00–15:00	15:00–17:00	17:00–19:00	19:00–21:00	21:00–23:00
1	○	●	○	●	◎	○	○	◎	○	●	○	●
2	●	○	○	◎	●	●	◎	○	○	◎	●	●
3	●	●	◎	◎	●	◎	○	○	◎	●	○	●
4	◎	◎	●	○	◎	◎	○	◎	●	●	○	●
5	○	●	◎	◎	◎	○	◎	○	●	○	●	●
6	●	○	◎	○	○	◎	●	○	○	○	○	◎
7	○	◎	○	○	◎	●	○	○	◎	●	◎	◎
8	◎	◎	○	○	●	●	○	●	○	◎	○	○
9	○	○	○	●	●	◎	○	●	○	◎	○	○
10	○	◎	●	○	◎	○	●	◎	○	●	○	○
11	◎	●	◎	◎	●	○	◎	◎	○	●	○	●
12	●	○	◎	○	●	○	◎	○	○	○	●	◎
13	●	◎	○	●	○	◎	◎	◎	◎	●	○	●
14	○	◎	●	◎	○	○	◎	◎	●	○	●	○
15	●	●	◎	◎	◎	◎	○	●	○	●	◎	○
16	◎	◎	◎	●	◎	◎	●	◎	●	○	◎	●
17	◎	○	◎	○	○	●	●	●	◎	○	●	◎
18	◎	●	○	◎	○	○	●	●	◎	◎	◎	◎
19	●	○	◎	○	●	◎	○	○	●	◎	◎	◎
20	○	◎	●	◎	○	○	○	○	◎	◎	●	●
21	◎	●	◎	◎	●	◎	●	○	◎	●	○	○
22	○	◎	○	●	◎	○	◎	○	●	○	○	○
23	○	●	◎	◎	●	◎	◎	○	○	○	○	○
24	●	○	○	○	◎	◎	○	○	●	◎	●	◎
25	○	○	●	◎	◎	◎	○	○	●	○	◎	○
26	○	○	◎	◎	●	●	●	◎	○	◎	●	●
27	○	○	◎	◎	●	●	○	○	◎	●	◎	●
28	◎	◎	●	●	●	○	●	◎	○	○	◎	○
29	◎	●	○	●	○	●	◎	◎	●	◎	●	◎
30	●	○	●	◎	○	○	●	○	◎	○	○	○
31	○	●	◎	●	○	●	◎	◎	○	●	◎	●

GOOD ◎   FAIR ○   BAD ●

APRIL　　　　　　　　　　　　　　　　　　　　　HOURS

	23:00–01:00	01:00–03:00	03:00–05:00	05:00–07:00	07:00–09:00	09:00–11:00	11:00–13:00	13:00–15:00	15:00–17:00	17:00–19:00	19:00–21:00	21:00–23:00
1	○	◎	○	○	●	●	◎	○	◎	◎	●	●
2	○	○	◎	◎	●	◎	○	●	◎	●	○	◎
3	◎	◎	○	○	◎	○	○	●	●	◎	◎	○
4	○	●	◎	◎	○	○	◎	●	●	○	○	●
5	●	○	◎	●	○	◎	●	○	○	◎	●	◎
6	○	◎	◎	●	●	●	○	◎	◎	●	◎	◎
7	◎	○	●	○	●	○	○	○	◎	◎	○	○
8	●	●	○	●	●	◎	◎	◎	◎	◎	◎	◎
9	○	◎	●	○	◎	◎	●	◎	◎	●	○	●
10	◎	●	◎	○	○	●	◎	◎	○	○	●	●
11	●	○	○	○	○	◎	◎	○	◎	○	●	◎
12	●	◎	○	●	○	◎	◎	◎	○	●	●	○
13	◎	◎	●	○	●	◎	○	●	◎	◎	●	●
14	○	○	○	◎	◎	◎	●	●	◎	●	○	○
15	○	◎	◎	●	◎	○	◎	●	○	○	◎	○
16	○	○	◎	◎	●	●	○	○	◎	○	○	○
17	◎	●	◎	●	●	○	●	●	◎	◎	○	◎
18	●	○	●	●	◎	○	◎	◎	○	◎	◎	◎
19	●	○	●	◎	○	○	○	○	◎	○	●	●
20	○	●	◎	◎	●	◎	○	◎	◎	●	◎	○
21	○	◎	●	●	◎	◎	◎	○	○	●	○	●
22	○	●	◎	○	○	◎	◎	○	○	●	○	○
23	●	○	○	○	◎	◎	○	○	○	○	○	◎
24	●	○	○	◎	◎	○	◎	○	●	●	◎	○
25	◎	◎	◎	○	●	●	●	○	○	○	●	●
26	○	○	◎	◎	●	◎	●	●	◎	●	○	●
27	◎	◎	○	●	○	●	◎	○	○	○	○	○
28	○	●	○	●	●	○	◎	◎	●	◎	○	○
29	●	○	○	○	◎	◎	●	○	◎	◎	●	○
30	○	●	○	●	◎	○	◎	○	●	○	○	●
31												

GOOD ◎　　FAIR ○　　BAD ●

MAY — HOURS

	23:00–01:00	01:00–03:00	03:00–05:00	05:00–07:00	07:00–09:00	09:00–11:00	11:00–13:00	13:00–15:00	15:00–17:00	17:00–19:00	19:00–21:00	21:00–23:00
1	●	○	○	◎	●	●	◎	○	○	◎	●	●
2	●	●	◎	◎	●	◎	○	○	◎	●	○	●
3	◎	◎	●	○	◎	◎	○	◎	●	●	○	●
4	○	●	◎	◎	◎	○	◎	○	●	○	●	●
5	●	○	◎	○	○	◎	●	○	○	○	○	◎
6	○	◎	○	○	◎	●	○	○	◎	●	◎	○
7	◎	◎	○	○	●	●	○	●	○	◎	○	○
8	○	○	○	●	●	◎	○	●	○	◎	○	◎
9	○	◎	●	○	◎	○	●	◎	○	●	○	◎
10	◎	●	◎	◎	●	○	◎	◎	○	●	○	●
11	●	○	◎	●	○	◎	◎	○	○	○	●	◎
12	●	◎	○	●	○	◎	◎	◎	○	●	◎	◎
13	○	◎	●	◎	○	○	◎	◎	●	○	●	◎
14	●	●	◎	◎	◎	◎	○	●	○	●	◎	○
15	◎	◎	◎	●	◎	◎	●	◎	●	○	◎	●
16	◎	○	○	○	○	●	●	●	◎	○	●	●
17	◎	●	○	●	○	○	●	●	◎	◎	◎	◎
18	●	◎	○	●	◎	○	◎	○	●	◎	◎	◎
19	○	◎	●	◎	○	○	○	○	◎	◎	●	●
20	◎	●	◎	◎	●	◎	●	○	◎	●	○	○
21	○	◎	○	●	◎	○	◎	○	○	○	○	○
22	○	●	◎	◎	●	◎	◎	○	○	○	○	○
23	●	○	○	○	◎	◎	○	○	●	◎	●	◎
24	○	○	●	◎	◎	◎	○	●	○	●	◎	○
25	○	○	◎	◎	●	●	●	◎	○	○	●	●
26	○	○	◎	◎	●	●	○	○	◎	●	◎	◎
27	◎	◎	●	●	●	○	●	◎	○	○	◎	○
28	◎	●	○	●	○	●	◎	◎	●	○	●	◎
29	●	○	●	◎	○	○	●	○	◎	○	○	○
30	○	●	◎	●	○	●	◎	◎	○	●	◎	●
31	○	◎	○	○	●	●	◎	○	◎	◎	●	●

GOOD ◎   FAIR ○   BAD ●

JUNE — HOURS

Day	23:00–01:00	01:00–03:00	03:00–05:00	05:00–07:00	07:00–09:00	09:00–11:00	11:00–13:00	13:00–15:00	15:00–17:00	17:00–19:00	19:00–21:00	21:00–23:00
1	○	○	◎	◎	●	◎	○	●	◎	●	○	◎
2	◎	◎	○	○	●	○	○	◎	●	●	◎	○
3	○	●	◎	◎	○	○	◎	●	●	○	○	●
4	●	○	◎	●	○	◎	●	○	○	◎	●	◎
5	○	◎	●	○	◎	●	○	○	◎	●	◎	◎
6	◎	○	●	○	●	○	○	○	◎	◎	○	○
7	●	●	○	●	●	◎	◎	○	◎	◎	◎	◎
8	○	◎	●	○	●	◎	●	◎	◎	●	○	●
9	◎	●	○	○	●	◎	◎	○	○	●	●	●
10	●	○	○	○	○	◎	◎	○	◎	○	●	◎
11	●	◎	○	●	○	◎	◎	◎	○	●	●	○
12	◎	◎	●	○	●	◎	○	●	◎	◎	●	●
13	○	○	○	◎	◎	◎	●	●	◎	●	○	○
14	○	◎	◎	●	◎	○	●	◎	●	○	◎	○
15	○	○	◎	◎	●	●	○	○	◎	○	○	○
16	◎	●	◎	◎	●	○	●	●	◎	◎	◎	◎
17	●	○	●	●	◎	○	◎	◎	○	◎	◎	◎
18	●	○	●	◎	○	○	○	◎	◎	◎	●	●
19	○	●	◎	◎	●	◎	○	◎	◎	●	◎	○
20	○	◎	●	●	◎	◎	◎	○	○	●	○	●
21	○	●	◎	○	○	◎	◎	◎	○	○	●	○
22	●	○	○	○	◎	◎	○	○	○	○	●	◎
23	●	○	○	◎	◎	○	◎	○	●	●	◎	○
24	◎	◎	◎	○	●	●	●	○	○	○	●	●
25	○	○	◎	◎	●	◎	●	●	◎	●	○	●
26	◎	◎	○	●	●	○	●	◎	○	○	○	○
27	○	●	○	●	●	○	◎	◎	●	◎	○	○
28	●	○	○	○	●	◎	●	○	◎	◎	●	○
29	○	●	○	●	◎	○	○	◎	○	●	○	●
30	●	○	○	◎	●	●	◎	○	○	◎	●	●
31												

GOOD ◎   FAIR ○   BAD ●

JULY   HOURS

Day	23:00–01:00	01:00–03:00	03:00–05:00	05:00–07:00	07:00–09:00	09:00–11:00	11:00–13:00	13:00–15:00	15:00–17:00	17:00–19:00	19:00–21:00	21:00–23:00
1	●	●	◎	◎	●	●	○	○	◎	●	○	◎
2	◎	◎	●	○	◎	◎	○	◎	●	●	○	●
3	○	●	◎	◎	◎	○	◎	○	●	○	●	●
4	●	○	◎	○	○	●	●	○	○	○	○	◎
5	○	◎	○	○	◎	●	○	○	◎	●	◎	◎
6	◎	◎	○	○	●	●	○	●	○	◎	○	○
7	○	○	○	●	●	◎	○	●	○	◎	○	◎
8	○	○	●	○	◎	○	●	◎	○	●	○	○
9	◎	●	◎	◎	●	○	◎	◎	●	○	●	○
10	●	○	◎	●	○	◎	◎	○	○	○	●	◎
11	●	○	○	●	○	◎	◎	◎	○	●	◎	◎
12	○	◎	●	◎	○	○	◎	◎	●	○	●	○
13	●	●	◎	◎	◎	◎	○	●	○	●	○	◎
14	◎	◎	◎	●	◎	◎	●	◎	●	○	◎	●
15	◎	○	◎	○	○	●	●	●	◎	○	●	◎
16	◎	●	○	●	○	○	●	●	◎	◎	◎	◎
17	●	◎	○	●	◎	○	●	○	●	◎	◎	◎
18	○	◎	●	◎	○	○	○	○	◎	◎	●	●
19	◎	●	◎	◎	●	◎	●	○	◎	●	○	○
20	○	◎	○	●	◎	○	●	○	○	●	○	○
21	○	●	◎	◎	●	◎	◎	○	○	○	○	○
22	●	○	○	○	◎	◎	○	○	●	●	◎	◎
23	○	○	●	◎	◎	◎	○	●	○	●	◎	○
24	○	○	◎	◎	●	●	●	◎	○	◎	●	●
25	○	○	◎	◎	●	●	○	○	◎	◎	◎	●
26	◎	◎	●	●	●	○	●	◎	○	○	◎	○
27	◎	●	○	●	○	●	◎	◎	●	◎	●	◎
28	●	○	●	◎	○	○	●	○	◎	○	○	○
29	○	●	◎	●	○	●	◎	◎	○	●	◎	●
30	○	◎	○	○	●	●	◎	○	◎	◎	●	●
31	○	○	◎	◎	●	◎	○	●	◎	●	○	◎

GOOD ◎   FAIR ○   BAD ●

AUGUST HOURS

	23:00–01:00	01:00–03:00	03:00–05:00	05:00–07:00	07:00–09:00	09:00–11:00	11:00–13:00	13:00–15:00	15:00–17:00	17:00–19:00	19:00–21:00	21:00–23:00
1	◎	◎	○	○	◎	○	○	◎	●	●	◎	○
2	○	●	◎	◎	○	○	◎	●	●	○	○	●
3	●	○	◎	●	○	●	○	○	◎	●	◎	◎
4	○	◎	●	○	◎	●	○	○	◎	●	◎	◎
5	◎	○	●	○	●	○	○	○	◎	◎	○	○
6	●	●	○	●	○	◎	◎	○	◎	◎	◎	◎
7	○	◎	●	○	●	◎	●	◎	◎	●	○	●
8	◎	●	◎	○	○	●	◎	◎	○	○	●	●
9	●	○	○	○	○	○	◎	○	◎	○	●	◎
10	●	◎	○	●	○	◎	◎	◎	○	●	●	○
11	◎	◎	●	○	●	◎	○	●	◎	◎	●	●
12	○	○	○	◎	◎	◎	●	●	◎	●	○	○
13	○	◎	◎	●	○	○	●	◎	●	○	◎	○
14	○	○	◎	◎	●	●	○	○	◎	○	○	○
15	◎	●	◎	●	●	○	●	●	◎	◎	○	◎
16	●	○	●	●	◎	○	◎	◎	○	◎	◎	◎
17	●	○	●	◎	○	○	○	◎	◎	◎	●	●
18	○	●	◎	◎	●	◎	○	○	◎	●	◎	○
19	○	◎	●	●	◎	◎	○	○	●	○	○	●
20	○	●	◎	○	○	◎	◎	○	○	●	○	○
21	●	○	○	○	◎	◎	○	○	○	○	○	◎
22	●	○	○	○	◎	○	◎	○	●	●	◎	○
23	◎	◎	◎	○	●	●	●	○	○	○	●	●
24	○	○	◎	◎	●	◎	●	●	◎	●	○	●
25	◎	◎	○	●	●	○	●	◎	○	○	○	○
26	○	●	○	●	●	○	◎	◎	●	◎	○	○
27	●	○	○	○	●	◎	●	○	◎	◎	●	○
28	○	●	○	●	◎	○	○	◎	○	●	○	●
29	●	○	○	◎	●	●	◎	○	○	◎	●	●
30	●	●	◎	◎	●	◎	○	○	◎	●	○	●
31	◎	◎	●	○	◎	◎	○	◎	●	●	○	●

GOOD ◎   FAIR ○   BAD ●

SEPTEMBER HOURS

	23:00–01:00	01:00–03:00	03:00–05:00	05:00–07:00	07:00–09:00	09:00–11:00	11:00–13:00	13:00–15:00	15:00–17:00	17:00–19:00	19:00–21:00	21:00–23:00
1	○	●	◎	◎	◎	○	◎	○	●	○	●	●
2	●	○	◎	○	○	◎	●	○	○	○	○	◎
3	○	◎	○	○	◎	●	○	○	◎	●	◎	◎
4	◎	◎	○	○	●	●	○	●	○	◎	○	○
5	○	○	○	●	●	◎	○	●	○	◎	○	◎
6	○	◎	●	○	◎	○	●	◎	○	○	○	○
7	◎	●	◎	◎	●	○	◎	◎	○	●	○	●
8	●	○	◎	●	○	◎	◎	○	○	○	●	◎
9	●	◎	○	●	○	◎	◎	○	●	◎	◎	◎
10	○	◎	●	◎	○	○	◎	◎	●	○	●	○
11	●	●	◎	◎	◎	◎	○	●	○	●	◎	○
12	◎	◎	◎	●	◎	◎	●	◎	●	○	◎	●
13	◎	○	◎	○	○	●	○	◎	○	◎	○	◎
14	◎	●	○	●	○	○	●	●	◎	◎	◎	◎
15	●	◎	○	●	◎	○	◎	○	●	◎	◎	◎
16	○	◎	●	◎	○	○	○	○	◎	◎	●	●
17	◎	●	◎	◎	●	◎	●	○	◎	●	○	○
18	○	◎	○	●	◎	○	◎	○	○	●	○	○
19	○	●	◎	◎	●	◎	◎	○	○	○	○	○
20	●	○	○	○	◎	◎	○	○	●	◎	●	◎
21	○	○	●	◎	◎	◎	○	●	○	●	◎	○
22	○	○	○	◎	●	●	●	◎	○	◎	●	●
23	○	○	◎	◎	●	●	○	○	◎	●	◎	◎
24	◎	◎	●	●	●	○	●	◎	○	○	◎	○
25	◎	●	○	●	○	●	○	●	◎	●	◎	○
26	●	○	●	◎	○	○	●	○	◎	○	○	○
27	○	●	◎	●	○	●	◎	◎	○	●	○	◎
28	○	◎	○	○	●	●	◎	○	◎	◎	●	●
29	○	○	◎	◎	●	◎	○	●	◎	●	○	◎
30	◎	◎	○	○	●	○	○	◎	●	●	◎	○
31												

GOOD ◎   FAIR ○   BAD ●

OCTOBER HOURS

Day	23:00–01:00	01:00–03:00	03:00–05:00	05:00–07:00	07:00–09:00	09:00–11:00	11:00–13:00	13:00–15:00	15:00–17:00	17:00–19:00	19:00–21:00	21:00–23:00
1	○	●	◎	◎	○	○	◎	●	●	○	○	●
2	●	○	◎	●	○	◎	●	○	○	◎	●	◎
3	○	◎	●	○	◎	●	○	○	◎	●	◎	◎
4	◎	○	●	○	●	○	○	○	◎	◎	○	○
5	●	●	○	●	●	◎	◎	○	◎	◎	◎	◎
6	○	◎	●	○	◎	◎	●	◎	◎	●	○	●
7	◎	●	◎	○	○	●	◎	◎	○	○	●	●
8	●	○	○	○	○	◎	◎	○	◎	○	●	●
9	●	◎	○	●	○	◎	◎	◎	○	●	◎	○
10	◎	◎	●	○	●	◎	○	●	◎	◎	●	●
11	○	○	○	◎	◎	◎	●	●	◎	●	○	○
12	○	◎	◎	●	◎	○	●	◎	●	○	◎	○
13	○	○	◎	◎	●	●	○	◎	○	○	○	○
14	◎	●	◎	●	●	○	●	●	◎	◎	○	◎
15	●	○	●	●	◎	○	◎	◎	○	◎	◎	◎
16	●	○	●	◎	○	○	◎	◎	◎	◎	●	●
17	○	●	◎	◎	●	◎	○	◎	◎	●	◎	○
18	○	◎	●	●	◎	◎	◎	○	○	●	○	●
19	○	●	◎	○	○	◎	◎	◎	○	○	●	○
20	●	○	○	○	○	◎	◎	○	○	○	○	◎
21	●	○	○	◎	◎	○	◎	○	●	●	◎	○
22	◎	◎	◎	○	●	●	●	○	○	●	●	●
23	○	○	◎	◎	●	◎	●	●	◎	●	○	○
24	◎	◎	○	●	●	○	●	◎	○	○	○	○
25	○	●	○	●	●	○	◎	◎	●	◎	○	○
26	●	○	○	○	◎	◎	●	○	◎	◎	●	○
27	○	●	○	●	◎	○	○	◎	○	●	○	●
28	●	○	○	◎	●	●	◎	○	○	◎	●	●
29	●	●	◎	◎	●	◎	○	○	◎	●	○	●
30	◎	◎	●	○	◎	◎	○	◎	●	●	○	●
31	○	●	◎	◎	◎	○	◎	○	●	○	●	●

GOOD ◎   FAIR ○   BAD ●

NOVEMBER   HOURS

Day	23:00–01:00	01:00–03:00	03:00–05:00	05:00–07:00	07:00–09:00	09:00–11:00	11:00–13:00	13:00–15:00	15:00–17:00	17:00–19:00	19:00–21:00	21:00–23:00
1	●	○	◎	○	○	◎	●	○	○	○	○	◎
2	○	◎	○	○	◎	●	○	○	◎	●	◎	◎
3	◎	◎	○	○	●	●	○	●	○	◎	○	○
4	○	○	○	●	●	◎	○	●	○	◎	○	◎
5	○	◎	●	○	◎	○	●	◎	○	●	○	○
6	◎	●	○	◎	●	○	◎	◎	○	●	○	●
7	●	○	◎	●	○	◎	◎	○	○	○	●	◎
8	●	◎	○	●	○	◎	◎	◎	○	●	◎	◎
9	○	◎	●	◎	○	○	◎	◎	●	○	●	○
10	●	●	◎	◎	◎	◎	○	●	○	●	◎	○
11	◎	◎	◎	●	◎	◎	●	◎	●	○	◎	●
12	◎	○	○	○	○	●	●	●	◎	○	●	◎
13	◎	●	○	●	○	○	●	●	◎	◎	◎	◎
14	●	◎	○	●	◎	○	◎	○	●	◎	◎	◎
15	○	◎	●	◎	○	○	○	○	◎	◎	●	●
16	◎	●	◎	◎	●	◎	●	○	◎	●	○	○
17	○	◎	○	●	◎	○	◎	○	○	●	○	○
18	○	●	◎	◎	●	◎	◎	○	○	○	○	○
19	●	○	○	○	◎	◎	○	○	●	◎	●	◎
20	○	○	●	◎	◎	◎	○	●	○	●	◎	○
21	○	○	○	◎	●	●	●	◎	○	●	◎	●
22	○	○	◎	◎	●	●	○	○	◎	●	◎	◎
23	◎	◎	●	●	●	○	●	◎	○	○	◎	○
24	◎	●	○	●	○	●	◎	◎	●	◎	●	◎
25	●	○	●	◎	○	○	●	○	◎	○	○	○
26	○	●	◎	●	○	●	◎	◎	○	●	◎	●
27	○	◎	○	○	●	●	◎	○	◎	◎	●	●
28	○	○	◎	◎	●	◎	○	●	◎	●	○	◎
29	◎	◎	○	○	◎	○	○	◎	●	●	◎	○
30	○	●	◎	◎	○	○	◎	●	●	○	○	●
31												

GOOD ◎   FAIR ○   BAD ●

DECEMBER   HOURS

	23:00–01:00	01:00–03:00	03:00–05:00	05:00–07:00	07:00–09:00	09:00–11:00	11:00–13:00	13:00–15:00	15:00–17:00	17:00–19:00	19:00–21:00	21:00–23:00
1	●	○	◎	●	○	◎	●	○	○	◎	●	◎
2	○	◎	●	○	◎	●	○	○	◎	●	◎	◎
3	◎	○	●	○	●	○	○	○	◎	◎	○	○
4	●	●	○	●	●	◎	◎	○	◎	◎	◎	◎
5	○	◎	●	○	◎	◎	●	◎	◎	●	○	●
6	◎	●	◎	○	○	●	◎	◎	○	○	●	●
7	●	○	○	○	○	◎	◎	○	◎	○	●	◎
8	●	◎	○	●	○	◎	●	◎	○	●	●	○
9	◎	◎	●	○	●	◎	○	●	◎	◎	●	●
10	○	○	○	◎	◎	◎	●	●	◎	●	○	○
11	○	◎	◎	●	◎	○	●	◎	●	○	◎	○
12	○	○	◎	◎	●	●	○	○	◎	○	○	○
13	◎	●	◎	●	●	○	●	●	◎	◎	○	◎
14	●	○	●	●	◎	○	◎	◎	○	◎	◎	◎
15	●	○	●	◎	○	○	○	◎	◎	◎	●	●
16	○	●	◎	◎	●	◎	○	◎	◎	●	◎	○
17	○	◎	●	●	◎	◎	◎	○	○	●	○	●
18	○	●	◎	○	○	◎	◎	◎	◎	○	●	○
19	●	○	○	○	◎	◎	○	○	○	○	○	◎
20	●	○	○	◎	◎	○	◎	○	●	●	◎	○
21	◎	○	◎	○	●	●	●	○	○	○	●	●
22	○	○	◎	◎	●	◎	●	●	◎	●	○	●
23	◎	◎	○	●	●	○	●	◎	○	○	○	○
24	○	●	○	●	●	○	◎	◎	●	◎	○	○
25	●	○	○	○	◎	◎	●	○	◎	◎	●	○
26	○	●	○	●	◎	○	○	◎	○	●	○	●
27	●	○	○	◎	●	●	◎	○	○	◎	●	●
28	●	●	◎	◎	●	◎	○	○	◎	●	○	●
29	◎	◎	●	○	◎	◎	○	◎	●	●	○	●
30	○	●	◎	◎	○	◎	○	●	○	●	●	●
31	●	○	◎	○	○	◎	●	○	○	○	○	◎

GOOD ◎   FAIR ○   BAD ●

Appendix
Your chinese animal sign

DATE OF BIRTH	CHINESE ANIMAL	DATE OF BIRTH	CHINESE ANIMAL
05.02.1936 - 03.02.1937	Rat	05.02.1980 - 03.02.1981	Monkey
04.02.1937 - 03.02.1938	Ox	04.02.1981 - 03.02.1982	Rooster
04.02.1938 - 04.02.1939	Tiger	04.02.1982 - 03.02.1983	Dog
05.02.1939 - 04.02.1940	Rabbit	04.02.1983 - 03.02.1984	Pig
05.02.1940 - 03.02.1941	Dragon	04.02.1984 - 03.02.1985	Rat
04.02.1941 - 03.02.1942	Snake	04.02.1985 - 03.02.1986	Ox
04.02.1942 - 04.02.1943	Horse	04.02.1986 - 03.02.1987	Tiger
05.02.1943 - 04.02.1944	Goat	04.02.1987 - 03.02.1988	Rabbit
05.02.1944 - 03.02.1945	Monkey	04.02.1988 - 03.02.1989	Dragon
04.02.1945 - 03.02.1946	Rooster	04.02.1989 - 03.02.1990	Snake
04.02.1946 - 03.02.1947	Dog	04.02.1990 - 03.02.1991	Horse
04.02.1947 - 04.02.1948	Pig	04.02.1991 - 03.02.1992	Goat
05.02.1948 - 03.02.1949	Rat	04.02.1992 - 03.02.1993	Monkey
04.02.1949 - 03.02.1950	Ox	04.02.1993 - 03.02.1994	Rooster
04.02.1950 - 03.02.1951	Tiger	04.02.1994 - 03.02.1995	Dog
04.02.1951 - 04.02.1952	Rabbit	04.02.1995 - 03.02.1996	Pig
05.02.1952 - 03.02.1953	Dragon	04.02.1996 - 03.02.1997	Rat
04.02.1953 - 03.02.1954	Snake	04.02.1997 - 03.02.1998	Ox
04.02.1954 - 03.02.1955	Horse	04.02.1998 - 03.02.1999	Tiger
04.02.1955 - 04.02.1956	Goat	04.02.1999 - 02.02.2000	Rabbit
04.02.1956 - 03.02.1957	Monkey	03.02.2000 - 03.02.2001	Dragon
04.02.1957 - 03.02.1958	Rooster	04.02.2001 - 03.02.2002	Snake
04.02.1958 - 03.02.1959	Dog	04.02.2002 - 03.02.2003	Horse
04.02.1959 - 04.02.1960	Pig	04.02.2003 - 03.02.2004	Goat
05.02.1960 - 03.02.1961	Rat	04.02.2004 - 03.02.2005	Monkey
04.02.1961 - 03.02.1962	Ox	04.02.2005 - 03.02.2006	Rooster
04.02.1962 - 03.02.1963	Tiger	04.02.2006 - 03.02.2007	Dog
04.02.1963 - 04.02.1964	Rabbit	04.02.2007 - 03.02.2008	Pig
05.02.1964 - 03.02.1965	Dragon	04.02.2008 - 03.02.2009	Rat
04.02.1965 - 03.02.1966	Snake	04.02.2009 - 03.02.2010	Ox
04.02.1966 - 03.02.1967	Horse	04.02.2010 - 03.02.2011	Tiger
04.02.1967 - 04.02.1968	Goat	04.02.2011 - 03.02.2012	Rabbit
05.02.1968 - 03.02.1969	Monkey	04.02.2012 - 03.02.2013	Dragon
04.02.1969 - 03.02.1970	Rooster	04.02.2014 - 03.02.2015	Horse
04.02.1970 - 03.02.1971	Dog	04.02.2015 - 03.02.2016	Goat
04.02.1971 - 04.02.1972	Pig	04.02.2016 - 02.02.2017	Monkey
05.02.1972 - 03.02.1973	Rat	04.02.2017 - 03.02.2018	Rooster
04.02.1973 - 03.02.1974	Ox	04.02.2018 - 03.02.2019	Dog
04.02.1974 - 03.02.1975	Tiger	04.02.2019 - 03.02.2020	pig
04.02.1975 - 04.02.1976	Rabbit	04.02.2020 - 02.02.2021	Rat
05.02.1976 - 03.02.1977	Dragon	03.02.2021 - 03.02.2022	Ox
04.02.1977 - 03.02.1978	Snake	04.02.2022 - 03.02.2023	Tiger
04.02.1978 - 03.02.1979	Horse	04.02.2023 - 03.02.2024	Rabbit
04.02.1979 - 04.02.1980	Goat	04.02.2024 - 02.02.2025	Dragon

Correcting the hour
solar time for major cities

CITY	CORRECTION	CITY	CORRECTION
Europe & Russia		Riga, Latvia	-23.32
Amsterdam, Holland	-40.28	Rome, Italy	-10.04
Athens, Greece	-25.08	Saint Petersburg, Russia	+01.00
Barcelona, Spain	+8.36	Samara, Russia	+20.36
Belgrade, Serbia	+21.48	Sarajevo, Bosnia-Herzeg.	+13.48
Berlin, Germany	-6.28	Seville, Spain	-24.00
Bern, Switzerland	-30.08	Skopje, FYROM	+25.40
Brussels, Belgium	-42.36	Sofia, Bulgaria	-26.40
Bucharest, Rumania	-15.36	Stockholm, Sweden	+12.12
Budapest, Hungary	+16.20	Stuttgart, Germany	-23.16
Cardiff, UK	-12.40	Tallinn, Estonia	-21.08
Chelyabinsk, Russia	+05.36	Tbilisi, Russia	-00.20
Copenhagen, Denmark	-9.40	Thessaloniki, Greece	-28.16
Dublin, Ireland	-25.00	Ufa, Russia	-16.20
Dusseldorf, Germany	-32.44	Valencia, Spain	-1.28
Edinburgh, UK	-12.44	Venice, Italy	-10.40
Frankfurt, Germany	-25.16	Vienna, Austria	+5.32
Geneva, Switzerland	-35.24	Vilnius, Lithuania	+41.08
Hamburg, Germany	-20.04	Warsaw, Poland	+24.00
Hannover, Germany	-21.04	Yekaterinburg, Russia	+02.32
Helsinki, Finland	-20.08	Zagreb, Croatia	+3.56
Kazan, Russia	+16.32	Zurich, Switzerland	
Kiev, Ukraine	+02.23		-25.52
Koln, Germany	-32.08	**North & South America**	
Las Palmas, Grand Canaria, S	-1.36	Acapulco, Mexico	-39.44
Lisbon, Portugal	-36.40	Atlanta, Georgia, USA	-37.32
Ljubljana, Slovenia	-1.56	Baltimore, Maryland, USA	-6.28
London, UK	0.00	Boston, Massachusetts, USA	+15.44
Lyon, France	+19.16	Bridgetown, Barbados	+1.32
Luxemburg, Luxemburg	-35.20	Buenos Aires, Argentina	+6.12
Madrid, Spain	-14.44	Calgary, Canada	-36.16
Manchester, UK	-9.00	Caracas, Venezuela	+2.20
Marseille, France	+21.32	Chicago, USA	+9.24
Milano, Italy	-23.12	Dallas, Texas, USA	-27.08
Minsk, Russia	-9.40	Denver, Colorado, USA	+0.04
Moscow, Russia	+30.20	Detroit, Michigan, USA	-32.12
Munich, Germany	-13.48	Edmonton, Canada	-34.00
Nice, France	+29.08	Habana, Cuba	-29.36
Nicosia, Cyprus	+13.28	Halifax, Canada	-14.20
Nizhniy Novgorod, Russia	-04.00	Honolulu, Hawaii, USA	-1.28
Novosibirsk, Russia	-28.28	Houston, Texas, USA	-21.32
Omsk, Russia	-06.24	Kingston, Jamaica	-7.12
Oslo, Norway	-17.04	La Paz, Bolivia	-32.36
Paris, France	+9.20	Las Vegas, Nevada, USA	+19.28
Prague, Czech. Republic	-2.16	Lima, Peru	-8.12
Reykjavik, Iceland	-27.48	Los Angeles, California, USA	+7.00

Correcting the hour
solar time for major cities

CITY	CORRECTION	CITY	CORRECTION
Miami, Florida, USA	-20.44	Jakarta, Indonesia	-23.00
Montevideo, Uruguay	-14.40	Karachi, Pakistan	-1h 01.52
Montreal, Canada	+5.44	Kobe, Japan	+0.44
Nassau, Bahamas	-9.20	Kuala Lumpur, Malaysia	-33.12
New York, New York, USA	+4.12	Kyoto, Japan	+3.00
Orlando, Florida, USA	-25.32	Manila, Philippines	+3.56
Ottawa, Canada	-2.48	Melbourne, Australia	-16.00
Panama City, Panama	-18.08	Muscat, Oman	-5.32
Philadelphia, Pennsylvania, USA	-0.44	Nagoya, Japan	+7.40
Pittsburgh, Pennsylvania, USA	-20.00	Nanking, Ku, China	-4.48
Quebec, Canada	+15.08	Okayama, Japan	-4.24
Quito, Ecuador	-14.00	Osaka, Japan	+1.56
Rio de Janeiro, Brazil	+7.00	Perth, Australia	-16.40
Santiago de Chile, Chile	-42.40	Phnom Penh, Cambodia	-0.32
San Diego, California, USA	+11.20	Port Louis, Mauritius	-10.00
San Francisco, California, USA	-9.44	Pyongyang, North Korea	-37.00
Sao Paolo, Brazil	-6.20	Rangoon, Burma	-5.24
Seattle, Washington, USA	-9.20	Sapporo, Japan	+25.16
Toronto, Canada	-17.28	Seoul, South Korea	-32.12
Vancouver, Canada	-12.28	Shanghai, China	+6.00
Washington DC, Virginia, USA	-12.40	Shenyang, China	-26.16
Winnipeg, Canada	-28.36	Singapore, Singapore	+45.00
		Sydney, Australia	+4.40
Asia, Middle East		Teheran, Iran	-4.16
& Australia		Taipei, Taiwan	-53.56
Adelaide, Australia	-15.40	Tel Aviv, Israel	+19.04
Amman, Jordanian	-36.16	Tokyo, Japan	+19.00
Ankara, Turkey	+11.20	Wellington, New Zealand	-20.52
Baghdad, Iraq	-2.24		
Bangalore, India	-19.36	Africa	
Bangkok, Thailand	-17.56	Addis Ababa, Ethiopia	-25.08
Beijing, China	-14.24	Alger, Algeria	+12.16
Brisbane, Australia	+12.08	Cairo, Egypt	+5.00
Brunei, Brunei	-20.12	Cape town, South Africa	-46.20
Calcutta, India	+23.20	Dar Es Salam, Tanzania	-7.52
Chengdu, Sz. China	-3.44	Johannesburg, South Africa	-7.52
Colombo, Sri Lanka	-10.28	Khartoum, Sudan	-10.08
Darwin, Australia	-46.44	Lagos, Nigeria	-46.28
Delhi, India	-21.04	Luanda, Angola	-7.04
Goa, India	-34.20	Mogadishu, Somalia	+1.24
Hangchow, Che, China	+0.40	Monrovia, Liberia	+0.48
Hanoi, Vietnam	+3.20	Mombasa, Kenya	-6.16
Hobart, Australia	-10.32	Nairobi, Kenya	-17.48
Ho Chi Min, Vietnam	+6.44	Rabat, Morocco	-27.24
Hong Kong, China	-23.24	Tananarive, Madagascar	+10.00
Istanbul	-4.08	Tripoli, Libya	-7.20
Izmir, Turkey	-11.28	Tunis, Tunisia	-19.20

The 24 mountains on the Feng Shui compass

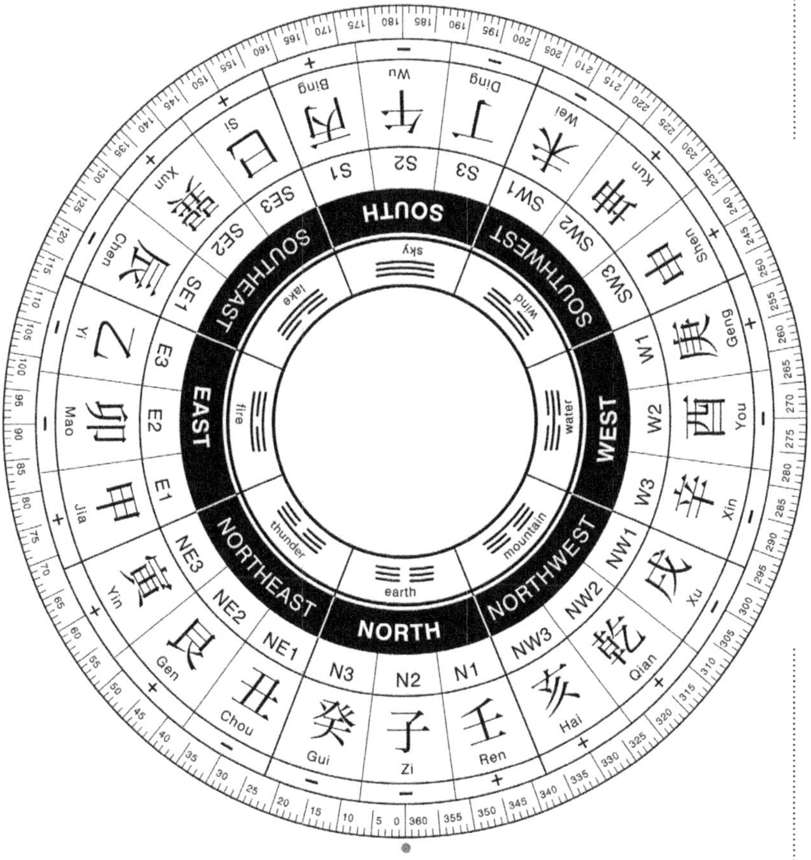

Master Georgia Kiafi

Georgia Kiafi is a professional Feng Shui & 4 Pillars of Destiny consultant. She is also an expert in I Ching Divination, Date Selection and Chinese Face Reading. Born in Athens - Greece, she speaks fluently 5 languages (greek, English, german, French and Italian) and travels around the world. She lives between Athens and Zurich.

Georgia is personally trained by Grand Master Raymond Lo from Hong Kong since they first met in 2000 in London. She worked with him during numerous Feng Shui and Destiny consultations around the world. She is now his European Associate. In 2015 she was recognised by the international Feng Shui Association as a Master in Feng Shui.

Georgia has appeared in Greek and Cypriot TV programs such as ANT1, Mega, Star, Alpha, Alter, RIK, Sigma etc. She has written articles and made predictions in many Greek newspapers and specialized magazines. She has given presentations in Switzerland, Greece, Germany, France, England, United Arab Emirates, Oman etc.

Georgia was a speaker at the International Feng Shui Convention in Singapore in 2006, the ideal Home Show in Dubai in 2006, the Feng Shui Festival in Singapore in 2007, the International Feng Shui Conference in 2006.

Website: www.thefengshuilife.com
Blog: georgiakiafi.blogspot.gr
Facebook Page: The Feng Shui Life

Printed in Great Britain
by Amazon